JANE AUSTEN : EMMA

by

FRANK W. BRADBROOK

Senior Lecturer in English,
University College of North Wales, Bangor

EDWARD ARNOLD (PUBLISHERS) LTD.
41 Maddox Street, London W.1

First published 1961
Reprinted 1963
Reprinted 1965
Reprinted 1967

Boards: SBN 7131 5056 4
Paper: SBN 7131 5057 2

Printed in Great Britain by Richard Clay (The Chaucer Press), Ltd.,
Bungay, Suffolk

General Preface

It has become increasingly clear in recent years that what both the advanced sixth former and the university student need most by way of help in their literary studies are close critical analyses and evaluations of individual works. Generalisations about periods or authors, general chat about the Augustan Age or the Romantic Movement, have their uses; but often they provide merely the illusion of knowledge and understanding of literature. All too often students come up to the university under the impression that what is required of them in their English literature courses is the referring of particular works to the appropriate generalisations about the writer or his period. Without taking up the anti-historical position of some of the American 'New Critics', we can nevertheless recognise the need for critical studies that concentrate on the work of literary art rather than on its historical background or cultural environment.

The present series is therefore designed to provide studies of individual plays, novels and groups of poems and essays, which are known to be widely studied in Sixth Forms and in universities. The emphasis is on clarification and evaluation; biographical and historical facts, while they may of course be referred to as helpful to an understanding of particular elements in a writer's work, will be subordinated to critical discussion. What kind of work is this? What exactly goes on here? How good is this work, and why? These are the questions which each writer will try to answer.

DAVID DAICHES

Contents

ACKNOWLEDGMENTS

I wish to thank Professor Michael Oakeshott, the General Editor, for permission to quote and adapt passages from two articles in *The Cambridge Journal*, 'Style and Judgment in Jane Austen's Novels' (Vol. IV No. 9), and 'The Letters of Jane Austen' (Vol. VII No. 5). My thanks are also due and gratefully given to Mr. J. C. Maxwell and the Editorial Department of *Notes and Queries*, published by the Oxford University Press, for permission to make use of material contained in two papers, 'Lord Chesterfield and Jane Austen' (February 1958) and 'Dr. Johnson and Jane Austen' (March 1960). Apart from the reference in the 'Select Bibliography', I should like to mention my indebtedness to the scholarship of Dr. R. W. Chapman, whose edition of the novels divides them into their separate volumes, as they were originally published.

NOTE

In the first edition of *Emma*, published by John Murray, there were eighteen chapters in the first and second volumes, and nineteen in the third. The title-page bears the date 1816, though the novel appeared in December 1815.

FRANK W. BRADBROOK.

ashen

STUDIES IN ENGLISH LITERATURE No. 3

General Editor
David Daiches
Fellow of Jesus College, Cambridge

1. The First Volume

Emma is the only major novel of Jane Austen that takes its title from the name of the heroine. The other characters who make up the society which the writer knew and which interested her are here strictly subordinated to the study of the education through experience which the protagonist undergoes. The theme of the young girl's entrance into society had been a conventional one in English fiction since Fanny Burney's *Evelina* (1778), but here Jane Austen is dealing with the rather different subject of the impingement of the outer world on a self-sufficient society in which the heroine is one of the dominating figures. Moreover, the heroine herself is by no means a conventional type of person. Jane Austen's nephew, J. E. Austen-Leigh states in his *Memoir* that 'she was very fond of Emma, but did not reckon on her being a general favourite; for, when commencing that work, she said, "I am going to take a heroine whom no one but myself will much like." '[1]

There is a series of letters written in a light-hearted spirit to her young niece Anna, which tells one something of the artistic problems which Jane Austen had to solve. Anna, herself, resembled, in certain respects, Catherine Morland, the common-sense heroine of *Northanger Abbey* who is led astray by her imagination, with whom Emma also shares many characteristics. 'No one who had ever seen Catherine Morland in her infancy, would have supposed her born to be a heroine,' *Northanger Abbey* opens. Catherine's prosaic, ordinary character is mockingly compared with the romantic ideal of heroism: 'to be disgraced in the eye of the world, to wear the appearance of infamy while her heart is all purity, her actions all innocence, and the misconduct of another the true source of her debasement, is one of those circumstances which peculiarly belong to the heroine's life, and her fortitude under it what particularly dignifies her character'.[2]

[1] *Memoir of Jane Austen*, ed. R. W. Chapman, p. 157.
[2] Chapter 8.

Emma, like Catherine in the earlier part of *Northanger Abbey*, represents an essentially anti-romantic view of heroism. We cannot
imagine her enduring 'the sleepless couch, which is the true heroine's
portion . . . a pillow strewed with thorns and wet with tears'.[1] It is
the fate of the romantic heroine to suffer and endure: it is Emma's
destiny to lose her complacency and suffer slightly, as she learns the
truth about herself and others.

The romantic conception of the heroine depended upon the naïve
division of humanity into good and bad. 'Till the heroine grows up,
the fun must be imperfect,'[2] Jane writes to Anna, because it is only
with maturity that the ironic mingling of good and bad becomes fully
apparent. 'Cecilia[3] is perhaps a little too solemn and good . . . her
want of Imagination is very natural'[4] is a criticism that might equally
be made of Fanny Price, the heroine of *Mansfield Park*, the novel that
preceded *Emma*. It is a criticism that could not be made of Emma herself, for she is as opposed to what may be called the puritan ideal, as
she is to the romantic. Pictures of perfection, Jane Austen said, made
her sick and wicked, and she was surprised to find that a character
could be both interesting and amiable. She criticised Anne Elliot, the
heroine of her own final, completed novel, *Persuasion*, because 'she is
almost too good for me'.[5]

While writing *Emma*, Jane Austen also produced, with the aid of
her friends, a *Plan of a Novel, according to hints from various quarters*. This
was inspired by various absurd suggestions of the librarian to the
Prince Regent, to whom Jane Austen had written asking for permission to dedicate *Emma* to his Royal Highness. It contains a brief sum-
mary of the characteristics of the conventional heroine against which
Jane Austen was reacting in *Emma*. 'Heroine a faultless Character
herself—, perfectly good, with much tenderness & sentiment, & not
the least Wit—very highly accomplished, understanding modern
Languages & (generally speaking) everything that the most accomplished young Women learn, but particularly excelling in Music—

---

[1] *Northanger Abbey*, Chapter 11.

[2] R. W. Chapman, *Jane Austen's Letters*, p. 401.

[3] A character in the story Anna was writing.

[4] R. W. Chapman, *Jane Austen's Letters*, p. 402.

[5] *Ibid.*, p. 487.

her favourite pursuit—& playing equally well on the Piano Forte & Harp—& singing in the first stile. Her Person, quite beautiful— dark eyes & plump cheeks. Book to open with the description of Father & Daughter—who are to converse in long speeches, elegant Language— & a tone of high, serious sentiment. . . . Throughout the whole work, Heroine to be in the most elegant Society & living in high style. The name of the work *not* to be *Emma*—but of the same sort as S & S. and P & P.'[1]

If one compares this with the opening of *Emma*, it might seem, at first glance, that the heroine follows the conventional pattern. She appears to be faultless, apart from a reference, in the fourth paragraph, to the evils which resulted from 'the power of having rather too much her own way'. (Later in the chapter, Mr. Knightley is introduced, 'one of the few people who could see faults in Emma Woodhouse, and the only one who ever told her of them'.) In order to appreciate the finer shades of Jane Austen's irony, however, one has to consider every word carefully. Emma has 'a comfortable home', and 'had lived nearly twenty-one years in the world with very little to distress or to vex her'. The adjective 'comfortable' is a danger signal, especially if one has just read *Mansfield Park*.

Lady Bertram, in *Mansfield Park*, is elderly, married and supremely 'comfortable': 'she had been a beauty, and a prosperous beauty all her life; and beauty and wealth were all that excited her respect'.[2] This is what Emma might have become (she is rich as well as handsome) if she had been less clever and inherited her father's indolence and vale-tudinarianism. Such an easy-going life is not Jane Austen's ideal, and Emma is to receive a series of severe shocks during the course of the novel. Experience, self-criticism and the criticism of others disturb her complacency with the result that she does not develop into the middle-aged 'comfortable' married woman, like Lady Bertram 'sunk back in one corner of the sofa, the picture of health, wealth, ease and tranquillity.'[3]

'You are now collecting your People delightfully,' Jane writes to her niece Anna, 'getting them exactly into such a spot as is the delight

[1] *The Minor Works*, ed. R. W. Chapman, pp. 428–430.

[2] *Mansfield Park*, Chapter 33.

[3] *Ibid.*, Chapter 15.

of my life;—3 or 4 Families in a Country Village is the very thing to
work on.'[1] The delicacy and precision with which Jane Austen
creates her picture of a society at the beginning of *Emma* is a mag-
nificent example of the controlled use of detail. Emma is nearly
twenty-one; Miss Taylor has taught and played with her since she
was five years of age; Miss Taylor's new home is half a mile away;
Emma's sister lives sixteen miles from Hartfield, in London; this
distance 'was much beyond her daily reach'; Highbury, the large and
populous village almost amounting to a town, really includes Hartfield, 'in spite of its separate lawn and shrubberies and name;' Mr.
Knightley is seven or eight-and-thirty; Mr. Elton is six or seven-and-
twenty, and has been vicar for a year. These are some of the things
that we learn in the first, brief chapter. The artistic economy of
means is accompanied by a lightness of touch in the moral discrimina-
tions made between the various characters, a lightness which can be
modified, however, and even become, at crucial moments in the
story, a devastating and direct moral judgment.

Between Emma and her governess Miss Taylor 'it was more the
intimacy of sisters'. This kind of 'substitute relationship' is frequently
found in the novels, and Miss Taylor had 'also fallen little short of a
mother in affection'. She replaces both the heroine's mother, who died
long before the story begins, and Isabella, her sister, who has married
Mr. Knightley's brother. The added complication of Miss Taylor's
marriage to Mr. Weston, and consequent removal, even if it is only
to a distance of half a mile, provides the initial dramatic situation.
Here one is made aware of the smallness of Jane Austen's world, the
way in which the little country town life is concentrated within itself
and separated from London, which is by modern means of communi-
cation so near. Within this physical, geographical self-centredness
there is a social 'in-breeding'. There is a sense in which the whole
community appears to be one large family. Whereas one may refer
vaguely today to 'the Family of Nations', or 'the Commonwealth
Family', Jane Austen's world is literally made up of closely-linked
family relationships. Frank Churchill, Mr. Weston's son by his first
wife, is the nephew and adopted heir of Mr. and Mrs. Churchill of
Enscombe in Yorkshire, but he comes to Hartfield and is expected to

[1] R. W. Chapman, *Jane Austen's Letters*, p. 401.

marry Emma. It is only when Mr. Elton is jilted that he makes the fatal mistake of going outside the community, and marrying Miss Augusta Hawkins, but he has not been in Highbury long enough to qualify as a native, and can hardly be expected to behave properly, for that reason. He never really belongs to 'the family', any more than he belongs to the place, and, ironically, the vicar, who should be 'the father of his parish' is the real 'outsider', together with his wife and the illegitimate Harriet Smith. Concentration on the unit of the small country town and the social drama of closely-knit family relationships is what gives Jane Austen's novels their artistic intensity and cleanness of dramatic impact, though the social range is wide, within these limitations.

Mr. Weston, whom Miss Taylor marries, 'was a native of Highbury, and born of a respectable family, which for the last two or three generations had been rising into gentility and property',[1] He is contrasted both socially and as a character with Mr. Knightley, who comes from an older, longer-established family, which shares with the Woodhouses pride of place in the hierarchy. He lacks the qualities of leadership and the tendency to dominate the community which are considered to be the natural result of social superiority. With his 'unexceptionable character, easy fortune, suitable age and pleasant manners'[2] he represents a social rather than a moral ideal, and though Jane Austen appreciates the social virtues, she is also acutely aware of the way in which too great sociability can lead to mediocrity and dullness. Mr. Weston has a warm heart like Miss Taylor, and this is the quality which unites them. Such characters are to be preferred to the various personifications of selfishness which are so subtly analysed by Jane Austen, but an individual such as Mr. Knightley represents qualities of independence and nonconformity to the conventions of society, which are regarded as superior. The debate about the comparative virtues of 'head' and 'heart' in human personality is what lies behind the distinction between these two characters. Harriet Smith, too, has a tender heart, and so, according to Emma, in a brief enthusiastic burst of sentimentality, have Mr. Woodhouse and Isabella.[3] Emma recognises, after her final mistake about Harriet's feelings has been made clear, 'the blunders, the blindness of her own head and

---

[1] Chapter 2.   [2] Chapter 1.   [3] Chapter 31.

heart! . . . To understand, thoroughly understand her own heart, was the first endeavour'.[1]

Though Jane Austen may have disliked pictures of perfection in her heroes and heroines, Mr. Knightley came as near her ideal as possible, an ideal which she summed up in one of her letters as a person 'where grace and spirit are united to worth, where the manners are equal to the heart and understanding'.[2] Mr. Weston, for all his attractiveness, has a hedonistic philosophy of 'eat, drink and be merry' which hardly satisfies the exacting standards of a writer who admired the stoicism of Dr. Johnson.

Mr. Knightley assumes a greater importance for Emma than he would otherwise do because her father is such an ineffectual figure. Mr. Woodhouse is 'beloved for the friendliness of his heart and his amiable temper', like Mr. Weston, but he is also old and a valetudinarian, without Mr. Weston's youthful social vivacity. His hatred of change and of marriage, which at first merely appears comic, in the end becomes sinister and frustrating, and the fact that his mind is as inactive as his body makes his company extremely boring. Emma's dutifulness towards him is one of the virtues that redeems her from her many faults, and we are presented with the ironical spectacle of the naturally gay, vivacious heroine enduring with fortitude a relationship which should be the source of her greatest pleasure. In such a situation, Mr. Knightley, whose age, 'seven or eight-and-thirty', is carefully noted, becomes, in certain respects, a substitute for the father who fails to provide his daughter with advice or congenial company, just as Miss Taylor had replaced the mother and sister whom she lost through death and marriage. Indeed, Mr. Woodhouse himself is only half-alive, and stands in the way of all the healthy vital instincts which issue in marriage.

Mr. Knightley's cheerfulness and physical vigour contrast with Mr. Woodhouse's pessimistic concern with his own and other people's health, just as his freedom from the more trivial aspects of life in provincial society is opposed to Mr. Weston's too easy-going sociability. Emma remarks to her father that Mr. Knightley 'loves to find fault with me'. The mingling of love and fault-finding is

[1] Chapter 47.
[2] R. W. Chapman, *Jane Austen's Letters*, p. 409.

characteristic, for he represents the point of view of a critical, formidable and shrewd male intellect, however affectionate he may be. In his relationship with Emma one can see reflected the traditional eighteenth century view of the virtues appropriate to men and women. Emma has imagination, generosity, intuition, social grace and charm, but Mr. Knightley's judgment of individuals, his ability to think, speak and act rationally and in a morally responsible way represents not merely the superiority of maturity but the natural dominating rôle of his sex in a society where men alone were regarded as being capable of thinking and acting seriously, and where women, however charming, were subservient. Emma, it is true, is the first lady in her little world; she is not afraid of defying Mr. Knightley, and even delights in organising other people's lives. But she is almost invariably proved to be wrong in her judgment of people and events, her defiance is rather that of the naughty spoilt child, and she suspects that Mr. Knightley may be right, even when she disagrees with him. The authority of Mrs. Weston herself is inferior to his. Only the vulgar Mrs. Elton assumes the right to address him familiarly, and considers that she is his equal.

Jane Austen could hardly envisage the sort of relationship that develops between Dorothea and Casaubon in George Eliot's *Middlemarch*. The relationship between Emma and her father, which gives the heroine her independence, is a reversal of the normal relationship between the sexes, as portrayed in Jane Austen's novels. An Elizabeth Bennet might be allowed to deliver a devastating snub to Darcy when he misbehaves in *Pride and Prejudice*, but once she recognises that he is a gentleman, she surrenders and only reserves the right to laugh at him occasionally.[1] Jane Austen certainly appreciates the ability of her sex to satirize and deflate masculine pomposity, but in her final novel, *Persuasion*, the heroine, Anne Elliot, states the inevitable limitations of the world in which her women characters live, when she remarks to Captain Harville, 'We cannot help ourselves. We live at home, quiet, confined, and our feelings prey upon us. You are forced on exertion. You have always a profession, pursuits, business of some

[1] The brilliant Mary Crawford in *Mansfield Park*, who attempts to dominate, is shown to be immoral and trivial.

sort or other, to take you back into the world immediately, and continual occupation and change soon weaken impressions.'[1] Captain Harville argues that there is an analogy between the physical and intellectual capabilities of men and women: 'our bodies are the strongest, so are our feelings, capable of bearing most rough usage, and riding out the heaviest weather.' Anne replies that men's feelings may be stronger, but that women's are more tender: 'Man is more robust than woman, but he is not longer-lived. . . . You have difficulties, and privations, and dangers enough to struggle with. You are always labouring and toiling, exposed to every risk and hardship.' The discussion which follows about the comparative constancy of the sexes concludes with Anne's comment that 'I believe you capable of every thing great and good in your married lives. I believe you equal to every important exertion, and to every domestic forbearance, so long as—if I may be allowed the expression, so long as you have an object. I mean, while the woman you love lives, and lives for you'. The appropriateness of such praise to Mr. Knightley becomes apparent as the story develops in *Emma*, but Anne's comment that 'All the privilege I claim for my own sex . . . is that of loving longest, when existence or when hope is gone' is only relevant to Jane Fairfax in *Emma*. The heroine herself is hardly a model of female constancy, and her little friend Harriet Smith is the personification of the traditional fickleness of her sex.

It may seem strange that Mr. Knightley should make his criticisms of Emma without her father's knowledge, as is stated in the opening chapter. 'We always say what we like to one another', Emma remarks, and in describing the wedding of Miss Taylor and Mr. Weston, there is an ironical anticipation of their own marriage, which concludes the novel. Their friendship already has the intellectual intimacy and freedom of marriage, but Emma has to be allowed to discover for herself through mistakes and blunders that her profoundest emotional relationship is also with Mr. Knightley. At the moment, she appears to be almost completely lacking in any significant emotional life. She is detached, witty, and interesting, with a suggestion, at times, of an element of hysteria in her wit which is a result of social embarrassment caused by inadequate company and

[1] *Persuasion*, Chapter 23.

lack of understanding by others. Her wit reminds one at times of Millamant, and when, towards the end of the novel she is described as being 'faultless in spite of all her faults',[1] Jane Austen repeats the words of Mirabell in Congreve's *The Way of the World*: 'I like her with all her faults; nay, I like her for her faults. Her follies are so natural, or so artful, that they become her; and those affectations which in another woman would be odious, serve but to make her more agreeable.'[2] Yet she is much less a woman of the world than Millamant, and Shakespeare's Rosalind, Viola and Beatrice have beneath the surface, verbal wit of their prose speech an emotional depth which finds its natural utterance in poetry. Jane Austen was no poet, however much she may have been indebted to *Twelfth Night* for the debate on women's constancy in *Persuasion*. Her strength and subtlety is in implying, analysing and leading up to the direct expression of emotion rather than in expressing emotion itself. Indeed, the direct expression of feeling is, for her, usually a sign of bad taste, and it is only at the end of her novels that she allowed her lovers to confess to each other. Then the moment is not dwelt on at length, but rather concentrated into one brief flash of speech or writing. Wit in *Emma* and silence in Mr. Knightley are the means by which they escape the emotional involvement with each other which would otherwise naturally develop. Mr. Knightley's intelligence also acts as a restraint, and it is only when Emma has achieved a similar maturity of intelligence that her wit transcends its limitations.

With Mrs. Perry, Mrs. and Miss Bates and Mrs. Goddard, one is introduced to the lower levels of society, the world of gossip and small-talk, which is also Mr. Woodhouse's, for he betrays his true responsibility by cultivating the company of the second-rate and stupid. The excuse for Emma's snobbery is that in her world the socially inferior characters are usually silly and dull, too. It is true that Fanny Price, the heroine of *Mansfield Park*, had been a good, poor girl who gained the reward of marriage with the hero as the result of simple virtue and modesty, and that in *Persuasion* Jane Austen introduces Mrs. Smith and Nurse Rooke who are poor and yet contrast favourably with the heroine's stupid, snobbish father and sister. In *Emma*, however, the heroine, who generally is snobbish, makes the

[1] Chapter 49.   [2] Act I, Scene III.

mistake of taking up Harriet Smith, who is poor like Fanny Price but also silly and illegitimate, and then trying to raise her from the society to which she belongs. It is the romantic aura of illegitimacy which appeals to Emma's imagination, and causes her to wreck the prospective marriage with Mr. Martin, the honest farmer and protégé of Mr. Knightley. This lower social world of *Emma* raises issues of manners and conduct which the novelist herself had obviously experienced in actual life. To what extent should social and intellectual inferiors be tolerated? Under what circumstances should one sacrifice such intelligence, taste and judgment as one possessed? Where was the line to be drawn between good manners, which, ideally, one should show to all, and the necessary assertion of one's independence? How could one reconcile a concern with truth and honesty in one's social relationships with the apparent toleration of mediocrity that good manners demanded?

Later in the novel one is introduced to Jane Fairfax, the only child of Mrs. Bates's younger daughter, who belongs by birth to Highbury. She has been given an excellent education. Mr. Knightley has told Emma that she sees in Jane the really accomplished young woman which she wanted to be thought herself. Jane Fairfax has to endure the inferior company of Mrs. and Miss Bates, just as Emma has to spend weary evenings with her father. Jane Fairfax would seem to be the natural friend for Emma, but instead she cultivates the more flattering company of Harriet Smith. The apparent lack of snobbery of the heroine in this particular case and the compassionate interest in the helpless, illegitimate girl are shown to be prompted by a desire to rule and dominate, which is merely one aspect of Emma's adolescent instability and uncertainty, while towards the gifted Jane Fairfax she shows a sense of inferiority.

Emma, who is clearly a spoilt child,[1] shows many of the symptoms of psychological disorder which are characteristic of the neurotic personality. Alfred Adler has remarked that the pampered child 'is granted prominence without working to deserve it, and he will

[1] It is interesting to compare J. Austen's treatment of this theme with that of George Eliot in *Daniel Deronda*, where Book I is entitled 'The Spoilt Child', and analyses the character of Gwendolen Harleth.

generally come to feel this prominence as a birthright'.[1] Emma maintains her prominence and attempts to rid herself of her feeling of inferiority by 'adopting' people and ruling their lives. Her neurotic daydreams are being constantly proved wrong, and her judgments of characters and the motives for people's actions are frequently mistaken in a manner that is typical in ordinary everyday life of this psychological type. Her boast at the beginning of the novel that she arranged the marriage between Miss Taylor and Mr. Weston 'and when such success has blessed me in this instance, dear papa, you cannot think that I shall leave off match-making' is a compensation of a neurotic personality suffering from inferiority feelings and uncertain of her own future. By this means her life is given a point and justification which it would not otherwise have, and she is released from the obsession with her father. It is as if she enjoys a vicarious courtship in arranging the marriages of other people, while her own anxiety is relieved in 'doing good'. Mr. Knightley is a gentleman-farmer, but he is also quite unconsciously, and without Jane Austen knowing it, a very efficient psychoanalyst. He immediately reduces her 'success' to its proper level: 'why do you talk of success? where is your merit?—what are you proud of?—you made a lucky guess; and *that* is all that can be said.' There is, however, a certain amount of animus in Mr. Knightley's rebuke. Perhaps he resents that marriage, which he is seriously considering, should be regarded so lightly by the young girl who is to become his wife. One cannot help sympathising with Emma's excuse, to a certain extent. Her life is so dull that one feels there is some reason for her 'bossiness'.

Education, particularly as it is reflected in the books that a person reads, but also including the various 'accomplishments' that young ladies were taught, is viewed with a certain degree of ironic detachment by Jane Austen, who had herself received little formal education. Emma's protégée, Harriet Smith, is being educated at Mrs. Goddard's school, 'a real, honest, old-fashioned Boarding-school, where a reasonable quantity of accomplishments were sold at a reasonable price, and where girls might be sent to be out of the way and scramble themselves into a little education, without any danger of coming back

[1] *What Life should Mean to You*, quoted by Lewis Way, *Alfred Adler: an Introduction to His Psychology*, p. 101.

B

prodigies'.[1] Harriet Smith, however, remains not merely stupid, but illiterate. Emma has to help her to write her letter refusing Mr. Martin: 'though Emma continued to protest against any assistance being wanted, it was in fact given in the formation of every sentence'.[2] Her conversation is similarly limited. Late on in the novel, the heroine has to listen to Harriet's reasons for believing that Mr. Knightley himself is fond of her: 'She listened with much inward suffering, but with great outward patience, to Harriet's detail.—Methodical, or well arranged, or very well delivered, it could not be expected to be; but it contained, when separated from all the feebleness and tautology of the narration, a substance to sink her spirit.'[3] Harriet is well-behaved, but when Emma first meets her 'she was not struck by any-thing remarkably clever in Miss Smith's conversation'. The appeal of Harriet to Emma is that she is helpless, easily impressed, willing to be led, affectionate and gives Emma the opportunity of improving her character, educating and training in taste and social discrimination.

Emma's first action, after the acquaintance has been made, is to at-tempt to break the relationship between Harriet and the family of the Martins of Abbey-Mill Farm, the neighbours of Mr. Knightley. Mr. Martin's reading, about which Emma enquires, shows that while he is not a formally educated man, he is not completely without culture. Harriet is vague about the exact extent of his reading, as she is about most things, but she has found out that he has not read all the fashionable horror and terror novels, which young ladies were ex-pected to know. While Emma is planning to educate her, she has started to debase the reading of the simple, honest farmer: 'He reads the Agricultural Reports and some other books, that lay in one of the window seats—but he reads all *them* to himself. But sometimes of an evening, before we went to cards, he would read something aloud out of the Elegant Extracts—very entertaining. And I know he has read the Vicar of Wakefield. He never read the Romance of the Forest, nor the Children of the Abbey. He had never heard of such books before I mentioned them, but he is determined to get them now as soon as ever he can.'[4]

Though Emma lives in such a small world, she says that she does not know Mr. Martin, an indication of the rigidity of the barriers of

[1] Chapter 3.   [2] Chapter 7.   [3] Chapter 47.   [4] Chapter 4.

class in Jane Austen's novels. Moreover, she does not want to know him, and the reason is not a mere snobbish one. Her coolness is due to the fact that he belongs to Mr. Knightley's world, and is, therefore, independent of her, and that he is not 'low' enough (as Harriet is) to allow her to be useful to him: 'a farmer can need none of my help, and is therefore in one sense as much above my notice as in every other he is below it'. She foresees (wrongly, of course) that his wife 'will probably be some mere farmer's daughter, without education', to which Harriet, showing some spirit, for once, does not agree. Harriet recognises that the Martins are quite as well educated as she is, and is very pleased with their company, until Emma interferes. Emma considers that he is not a gentleman, he is lacking in 'manner'. His lack of education is merely one aspect of his lack of breeding. It is necessary to be a gentleman, though there are degrees of gentility, a hierarchy descending from Mr. Knightley and Mr. Woodhouse, to Mr. Weston, then (at the moment) Mr. Elton, with Mr. Martin beyond the pale, outside 'society'. 'Manner', which is the manner the gentlemen have 'of carrying themselves; of walking; of speaking; of being silent', is what makes the difference. Loudness, coarseness and awkwardness, which can be forgiven in the young, are inexcusable in the old. Mr. Martin is awkward and abrupt, and will become, Emma thinks, 'a completely gross, vulgar farmer— totally inattentive to appearances, and thinking of nothing but profit and loss'.

One notes how Emma and Harriet's discussion of Mr. Martin defines in a most precise and delicate way, a general conception of good manners, though Emma's judgment of him is mistaken and her opinion contrasts with that of Mr. Knightley, which follows. Even Harriet unconsciously deflates Emma's prejudice, when she agrees submissively that it is very bad to think of nothing but profit and loss. Emma herself is inclined to be materialistic, and behind the reference there is the further irony of the biblical use of the word 'profit': 'What is a man profited, if he shall gain the whole world, and lose his own soul?' Jane Austen occasionally suggests in *Emma* the profounder irony of the contrast between the ordinary prosaic world and religious experience which had been one of the themes of *Mansfield Park*, though one could never expect any of her characters to achieve the intensity of religious experience of T. S. Eliot in *Ash Wednesday*.

> Wavering between the profit and the loss
> In this brief transit where the dreams cross
> The dreamcrossed twilight between birth and dying.

It would be a mistake, however, to assume because the work of Jane Austen is so prosaic that she was unacquainted with poetry and un-interested in religion. Professor C. S. Lewis has stated that he has come 'to regard the greatest of all divisions in the history of the West that which divides the present age from, say, the age of Jane Austen and Scott',[1] and has written persuasively illustrating the implied and specific religious content in Jane Austen's novels, generally.[2] Her stories, in certain respects, tended to follow the older moralistic and allegorical patterns, as those of Bunyan had done in the seventeenth century.

Emma remarks to Harriet that the fact that Mr. Martin is 'illiterate and coarse need not disturb *us*', though Harriet is illiterate too, and even Emma is hardly qualified for the rôle of guide, philosopher and friend that she assumes. Harriet regards Mr. Martin's lack of interest in 'The Romance of the Forest' and 'The Children of the Abbey' as an unamiable flaw in his character, while Emma tries to direct her attention from him by continuing her comparison and contrast of the manners of Mr. Elton, Mr. Weston and Mr. Knightley. Emma's in-tention is to replace Mr. Martin by Mr. Elton in Harriet's regard, but her praise of him as a model is later to be proved by his behaviour to be completely mistaken. Emma considers that Mr. Elton is 'quite the gentleman', though not of a sufficiently high social standing to object to Harriet's illegitimacy. Her praise is really modified by a certain degree of contempt, his virtues being mainly negative, 'a young man whom any woman not fastidious might like', and by her attitude towards Mr. Elton Emma shows that she really despises Harriet, too, despite her apparent eagerness and enthusiasm to help her. Harriet is too good for Mr. Martin, but she is good enough for

[1] *De Descriptione Temporum*, An Inaugural Lecture, p. 11.

[2] 'A Note on Jane Austen', *Essays in Criticism*, Vol. IV, No. 4, Oct. 1954.

the mediocre, inelegant Mr. Elton, whose apparently perfect manners are, in their turn, good enough for his station in life. This contempt for 'the cloth' which appears to be so cynically at variance with Jane Austen's professed and real religious beliefs, must be viewed historically. In the eighteenth century, to which Jane Austen essentially belongs on this kind of issue, there is no inconsistency in both despising the actual religious practice and paying conventional respect to the profession of the clergyman. Jane Austen, like Swift, could, no doubt, have produced 'an argument to prove that the abolishing of Christianity may be attended with some inconveniences'.[1] She accepted the fact that society was only nominally Christian, as Swift had suggested in his 'Argument'.

Such 'damning with faint praise' is frequently to be found in Jane Austen. In the next chapter, she immediately heightens the contrast between the heroine and the secondary characters by introducing a discussion of Emma by Mr. Knightley and Mrs. Weston, two persons who really do represent a model and a standard of manners and morals. Mrs. Weston is in favour of this new friendship between the heroine and Harriet Smith. Mr. Knightley is sceptical about Emma's qualifications as an educator, and sees in her intellectual slackness an indication of a more general feebleness of character. She is without industry and patience and cannot subject the fancy to the understanding. Mr. Knightley is valiant-for-truth in an almost Puritanical, Bunyanesque sense, though he is also the Mr. Great-Heart of this *Pilgrim's Progress*. His affection is modified by his judgment, and his judgment is exercised on behalf of a stern, unbending moral concern for Emma's future. Emma was so much the cleverer of the two sisters that she has been encouraged from an early age to consider herself cleverer than everyone else, and the friendship with Harriet is exactly what she needs to confirm herself in this opinion. Emma, as Mr. Knightley sees her, is 'lacking in strength of mind', the personification of feminine irrationality, while there is even a slight condescension in Mrs. Weston's reference to 'dear Emma's little faults' and the description of her as an 'excellent creature'.

[1] Swift's 'Argument' was praised by Johnson as 'a very happy and judicious irony', in his life of Swift. *The Lives of the English Poets*, by Dr. Johnson, influenced Jane Austen in many ways.

Mr. Knightley's disinterested criticism of Emma is followed by Mr. Elton's flattering praise of the way she is improving Harriet's character. There is a kind of vicious circle of flattery and self-deception here. Emma, pleasing Harriet by her interest and company is, in her turn, flattered by the response. Mr. Elton's praise is meant for her, not for Harriet, and Emma responds by directing Mr. Elton's attention to the numerous, innate virtues of Harriet and suggests, self-depreciatingly, that her help was not really necessary, except to give her 'a little more decision of character', and in order to teach her 'to think on points which had not fallen in her way before'. Emma, in other words, is claiming that she is giving Harriet that 'strength of mind' which Mr. Knightley has just denied that she is capable of giving. Mr. Elton's flattery of Emma when she attempts a drawing of Harriet completes the circle of mistaken motives and deception.

The sly, unobtrusive skill with which Mr. Elton is sent off to London to get the drawing framed, while Emma, Harriet and Mr. Knightley between them conclude the episode of Mr. Martin's courtship, is an example of Jane Austen's control over the dramatic development of the story. It is a very odd coincidence that Mr. Martin should propose on the very same day that Mr. Elton goes to London, but the relationships between the characters are by now so complicated and delicately balanced that few readers notice the unlikelihood of the events occurring in just the way that they do. This lack of realism in a writer who is usually so meticulously realistic almost amounts to a dramatic convention, and results in the reader's attention being constantly shifted as different combinations of characters appear. One has not forgotten about Mr. Martin, but he has begun to fade from one's immediate consciousness, and the sudden proposal is like the dramatic re-entrance of a character on the stage. But Mr. Martin's proposal is, in fact, merely a means of developing further the relationship between Emma and Harriet and of accentuating the different opinions of Emma and Mr. Knightley which lead to an explosion of hostility and anger between them. Emma, in Mr. Knightley's opinion, has made a radical mistake in considering that it is 'a degradation to illegitimacy and ignorance, to be married to a respectable, intelligent gentleman-farmer'. She has made the double error of believing that Harriet is superior socially and intellectually. Emma's defence is that Harriet is beautiful and good-tempered, two most important merits in a wife. To which Mr. Knightley replies that 'vanity working on a weak head, produces every sort of mischief', that men are not so fond of stupid wives as Emma thinks, and that 'Robert Martin's manners have sense, sincerity, and good-humour to recommend them; and his mind has more true gentility than Harriet Smith could understand'. He concludes by warning Emma that if she is thinking of Mr. Elton as a prospective husband for Harriet, she will be disappointed. Mr. Elton is too worldly and prudent, and 'knows the value of a good income as well as anybody'. Emma's view that Mr. Knightley has underrated Mr. Elton's passion is ironical in view of the fact that it is directed towards herself, and is soon to reveal itself to her great embarrassment and rage. Her remark to Harriet, when she thinks that Mr. Elton is courting her friend, that 'we are not to be addressing our conduct to fools', also has unconsciously comic reverberations.

As Mr. Martin fades out of view again, the interest of the reader is aroused by the introduction of Mr. John Knightley, his wife Isabella, and their five children (it is, perhaps, appropriate that one of them should be called Emma). After the debate on marriage, the resolution of the Martin crisis, the development of the Elton intrigue, what could be more natural than to introduce a large family to show practically what marriage is like, after the theoretical discussion? First, however, Emma gives Harriet her reasons for not wanting to marry, makes the important point that 'it is poverty only which makes celibacy contemptible to a generous public!' and describes an imaginary middle-aged life of spinsterhood that bears a close resemblance to that of Jane Austen herself. Perhaps it is not a mere coincidence that Emma has 'the true hazel eye'[1]: J. E. Austen-Leigh says that Jane Austen had 'bright hazel eyes'.[2] Only Jane's family and friends, who formed a specially privileged audience within the larger, general public who read and admired the novels, would see the joke. They must have appreciated much more keenly than the present-day reader the element of self-satire in the novel. Jane Austen is both mocking herself and indulging in a wish-fulfilment dream of the marriage that she herself was never to experience and enjoy.

[1] Chapter 5.   [2] *Memoir of Jane Austen*, ed. R. W. Chapman, p. 87.

Mr. Woodhouse 'could not think so ill of any two persons' under-standing as to suppose they meant to marry till it were proved against them',[1] and the comic selfishness of his attitude to marriage is clear. On the other hand, as a spinster, Jane Austen supports the dig-nity of the unmarried life in Emma's vision of her future as a mere aunt. The visit that Emma pays to the poor sick family, the charity and compassion that she shows, together with the reflection that 'these are the sights, Harriet, to do one good', also suggest personal experience by Jane Austen herself, and hardly seem consistent with the character who shows such contempt for Mr. Martin. To respect the poor, and despise the moderately wealthy and independent, hardly seems an attitude based on true Christian charity. One is not allowed, at this particular moment, to think of poverty for long, in any case. Mr. Elton interrupts Emma's moralising reflections. The comedy of the character and speech of Miss Bates, which looks for-ward to that of Dickens or James Joyce, exists independently of her poverty.

Mr. and Mrs. John Knightley represent a variation on the themes that have already been introduced. Jane Austen is always at her best in showing the similarities, differences and inter-connections between members of a family, since she is really exercising in her art the same powers of analysis and appreciation that the visits to her brothers and their families must have provoked in actual life. Mrs. John Knightley is a lady, but 'she was not a woman of strong understanding or any quickness'. Mr. Knightley has said to Mrs. Weston that Emma's 'education' of Harriet does not 'give any strength of mind', but, generally speaking, Emma contrasts with her sister, who resembles Mr. Woodhouse in her valetudinarianism, general benevolence, and dislike of change. These similarities and differences are balanced by the comparison and contrast between Mr. Knightley and his brother John, who is clever and formidable, too, but without the gracious-ness and courtesy of the gentleman-farmer. Mr. John Knightley lives in London, and has some of the slickness and hardness which Jane Austen seems to have regarded as essential for success in the big city.[2]

[1] Chapter 23.
[2] Though in *Pride and Prejudice*, Mr. Gardiner 'lived by trade, and within view of his own warehouses' in London, and yet is well bred and agreeable.

Her own favourite brother Henry was a banker in London, and went bankrupt three months after the appearance of *Emma*.

With the introduction of Mr. and Mrs. John Knightley in Chapter 11, there is also a mention of Frank Churchill, who has not been referred to since the second chapter, and who is not to appear until Chapter 23, though he is discussed in Chapter 18. The way in which Jane Austen prepares for the entrance of Mr. Knightley's rival, and times it just as Mr. Elton fades out, exemplifies that unobtrusive almost instinctive skill of the mature artist. The same masterly timing is shown in the introduction of Jane Fairfax in Chapter 20, between the discussion of Frank Churchill's character and his actual arrival. The delicacy of discrimination of character in Jane Austen sometimes reminds one of a finely balanced watch: the entrance and departure of the characters resemble the moves of an expert chess-player. The appearance of Jane Fairfax and Frank Churchill, the most important of the secondary characters, is carefully and shrewdly reserved for the crucial second, central volume.

The relationship between Mr. Knightley and his brother seems to represent Jane Austen's ideal for friendship between men. What she admires in the masculine world is its understatement and reserve, which contrast so favourably with feminine diffuseness and sentimentality. The very style of speech differentiates the two sexes, and in Mr. Knightley and his brother's greetings to each other, we have the brief exchange of two 'strong, silent men' (for Jane Austen believes in this convention) whose clichés conceal their subtlety and cunning, just as their brevity conceals their capacity for action, power and strength. They are two shrewd businessmen, eyeing their friends as so many social cattle, crops or clients (Mr. John Knightley is a lawyer), and without any intention of wasting time or words even in their greetings, and yet genuinely fond of their friends and of each other: ' "How d'ye do, George?" and "John, how are you?" succeeded in the true English style, burying under a calmness that seemed all but indifference, the real attachment which would have led either of them, if requisite, to do every thing for the good of the other.' Such reticence in personal relationships is like the proverbial still waters, revealing depth and sincerity of feeling, and contrasting with the hysteria, insincerity and gush of romantic

feminine friendship. Mr. John Knightley's rudeness to his wife is skil-
fully covered up by Emma, just as his temper at Mr. Woodhouse's
advice about the virtues of Cromer as a sea-bathing place, is
cleverly diverted by his brother. In the midst of the new tensions
that inevitably arise as a result of this addition to society, Emma and
Mr. Knightley show a superior poise and graciousness. They are
socially allies again, after their previous disagreement.

Now that a sufficiently large group of people has been collected,
a party is needed to gather them together, but Jane Austen avoids the
obvious. Just as Mr. Martin's proposal coincides with Mr. Elton's
departure to London, so Harriet's absence from the party at the
Westons' on Christmas Eve, due to a cold and sore throat, allows Mr.
Elton to confess his passion to Emma in the carriage while they are
returning. The party also brings Emma and Mrs. Weston together
and allows them to discuss 'all the little matters on which the daily
happiness of private life depends', which play such an important part
in Jane Austen's novels. It is also appropriate that in this party which
is to conclude the ambiguous relationship between Emma and Mr.
Elton, Frank Churchill's name should be brought up again, and
Emma's feelings towards him made clear: 'Now it so happened that
in spite of Emma's resolution of never marrying, there was something
in the name, in the idea of Mr. Frank Churchill, which always
interested her. She had frequently thought—especially since his
father's marriage with Miss Taylor—that if she *were* to marry, he
was the very person to suit her in age, character and condition. He
seemed by this connection between the families, quite to belong to
her. She could not but suppose it to be a match that every body who
knew them must think of. That Mr. and Mrs. Weston did think of
it, she was very strongly persuaded; and though not meaning to be
induced by him, or by any body else, to give up a situation which she
believed more replete with good than any she could change it for, she
had a great curiosity to see him, a decided intention of finding him
pleasant, of being liked by him to a certain degree, and a sort of
pleasure in the idea of their being coupled in their friends' imagina-
tions.' It is against this background of an increasing awareness of
the approaching meeting with Frank Churchill, and of all that is to
be said in his favour, that Mr. Elton makes his ill-timed advances.

Mr. Elton makes the mistake of assuming that he has 'the right of interest in her'. To be ill-bred in Jane Austen's world is to over-reach oneself, to step outside the proper limits established by custom. In *Pride and Prejudice* Darcy assumes too easily that Elizabeth will accept him and is informed that nothing would ever persuade her to accept, even if he had behaved more like a gentleman. But Darcy is a gentleman and can redeem himself. Mr. Elton's lack of inhibition and reserve, his complacent assumption and indelicate forcing of attention prove that he is not a gentleman. There are occasions when words are inadequate to express one's feelings, and Emma 'could only give him a look; but it was such a look as she thought must restore him to his senses'. Mr. Elton, however, remains extremely wild, and confesses his love to her in a gross and direct manner in the carriage on the way back from the party, thus confirming his lack of breeding.

Mr. Elton is a social-climber as well as an intruder into society, and his motives in courting the heroine are purely mercenary and materialistic. His confidence has been heightened by Mr. Weston's good wine, and his bewilderment and rage are all the greater when he discovers that Emma considers that he is only worthy to marry Harriet. Emma's fury is equally great when she finds that he thinks that he is worthy to marry herself. The mutual frustration is intensi-fied by the fact that they cannot escape from each other's company. The claustrophobia natural and inevitable in provincial society, here reaches its climax: 'if there had not been so much anger, there would have been desperate awkwardness; but their straightforward emotions left no room for the little zigzags of embarrassment'.[1] The vicar, whose marriage Emma so altruistically planned in the first chapter ('this is the only way I have of doing him a service') manages finally to control himself, and withdraws. We are informed three pages later that Emma is the heiress of thirty thousand pounds, and the motives for Mr. Elton's wishing to marry her are clear. Mr. Knightley had interpreted Mr. Elton's character correctly at the end of the first chapter and later told her that the vicar would never marry im-prudently. His brother warned Emma of his suspicions that it was herself and not Harriet whom Mr. Elton was courting. 'There was no denying that those brothers had penetration', while Mr. Elton is

[1] Chapter 15.

'proud, assuming, conceited; very full of his own claims, and little concerned about the feelings of others', understanding the gradations of rank below him, and blind to what rose above. Emma has made the same mistake with Harriet and Mr. Elton that she committed in the remarks about match-making in the opening chapter: 'It was adventuring too far, assuming too much, making light of what ought to be serious, a trick of what ought to be simple.'

In the final chapter of the first volume Emma announces to Mr. Knightley the postponement of the visit of Frank Churchill (Chapter 18), when she is still upset by the collapse of her plan for the marriage between Harriet and Mr. Elton. At the moment, she is not very interested whether Frank Churchill comes or not, but, being something of an actress, she pretends to be indignant with his rich aunt and uncle for keeping him away, praises him more than she normally would, and defends him for his apparent negligence. In doing so, she completely contradicts what she has said in a conversation with Mrs. Weston in Chapter 14 (that he really could come if he wanted to). This is what Mr. Knightley now maintains, but Emma, owing to her temporary nervousness and real indifference, reacts and pretends to support the view that Mrs. Weston had maintained in the earlier chapter, that his dependence on his rich relations does not allow him freedom of choice. Jane Austen's skill in showing the way in which, with the changes in her heroine's emotional state, her opinions and ideas alter, so that she is, strictly speaking, guilty of contradicting herself or of lying, is one aspect of the general psychological realism and insight characteristic of the novel.

Mr. Knightley's opinion that Frank Churchill is probably 'proud, luxurious and selfish', though containing elements of truth, is biased, as is his general judgment of Frank Churchill's character. Between Mr. Knightley and Frank Churchill there is the instinctive antipathy of completely opposite types of personality, further accentuated, in Mr. Knightley's case, by fear and sexual jealousy. Yet Mr. Knightley is correct when he argues that Frank Churchill is probably amiable, weak and a follower of expediency. To these failings, he opposes the ideas of resolution, a sense of duty, manliness and reason, which he himself embodies. Emma suggests that he may be of a more yielding, complying and mild disposition than Mr. Knightley, but she does not see this as necessarily a fault. When Mr. Knightley accuses Frank Churchill of falsehood, there is unconscious irony: for Emma has been lying, too. There is a sense in which Emma and Mr. Knightley are both right and prejudiced in their judgments, just as there is a sense in which Frank Churchill is both pleasant and attractive in his manners and trivial and reprehensible in his morals. What Jane Austen is clearly indicating is the way in which Frank Churchill naturally appeals to the superficial side of Emma's nature, with which he has a good deal in common, while the strength and worth of the heroine, which she shares with Mr. Knightley, only emerge as a result of suffering and disillusionment with herself and others.

Frank Churchill himself embodies the classical ideal of 'suaviter in modo, fortiter in re' (gentle in manner, resolute in deed) recommended by Lord Chesterfield in his *Letters to His Son*, the standard eighteenth century conduct book for young gentlemen, together with the modern French equivalent of 'douceur' and the cultivation of the "aimable" that Lord Chesterfield also inculcated. When Mr. Knightley passes judgment on his youthful rival, he remarks that Frank Churchill 'can be amiable only in French, not in English. He may be "aimable", have very good manners, and be very agreeable; but he can have no English delicacy towards the feelings of other people: nothing really amiable about him'.[1] Lord Chesterfield intended to make his son 'both *respectable et aimable*, the perfection of a human character',[2] and frequently referred to the necessity of cultivating the Graces, which 'seem to have taken refuge in France'.[3] Frank Churchill says that he is 'sick of England—and would leave it tomorrow, if I could',[4] a statement that reflects his French dandyism and the Chesterfieldian code of manners which provided Jane Austen with a model for the villain of her novel. Yet the graciousness of the eighteenth century aristocratic code, the polish which contrasted so favourably with the crudities of provincial life, inevitably had its attractions for Jane Austen, and the tension at the heart of the novel is created by the struggle in the heroine's mind between this ideal and

---

[1] Chapter 18.
[2] *Letters to His Son*, London, November 8, O.S. 1750.
[3] *Ibid*, November 18, O.S. 1748.
[4] Chapter 42.

the more rugged, native tradition of morals and manners, represented by Mr. Knightley.

The realism of Lord Chesterfield, his cynicism and disenchanted worldly wisdom appealed to Jane Austen, yet there was a fundamental disagreement between them about the moral principles that should guide human beings in their social relationships. Lord Chesterfield observed that 'Good manners, to those one does not love, are no more a breach of truth, than "your humble servant" at the bottom of a challenge is; they are universally agreed upon and understood to be things of course. They are necessary guards of the decency and peace of society; they must only act defensively; and then not with arms poisoned with perfidy. Truth, but not the whole truth, must be the invariable principle of every man who hath either religion, honour, or prudence. Those who violate it may be cunning, but they are not able. Lies and perfidy are the refuge of fools and cowards'.[1] Mr. Knightley, on the other hand, is not content with anything less than the whole truth, and in condemning Frank Churchill, he condemns, by implication, the point of view of Lord Chesterfield: 'Always deceived in fact by his own wishes, and regardless of little besides his own convenience.—Fancying you to have fathomed his secret.—Natural enough!—his own mind full of intrigue, that he should suspect it in others.—Mystery; Finesse—how they pervert the understanding! My Emma, does not every thing serve to prove more and more the beauty of truth and sincerity in our dealings with each other?'[2] The relationship between Jane Fairfax and Frank Churchill is an example of that duplicity that Lord Chesterfield accepted as inevitable in social relationships. Jane Austen does not accept it, and she makes her protest through the mouth of Emma: 'So unlike what a man should be! None of that upright integrity, that strict adherence to truth and principle, that disdain of trick and littleness, which a man should display in every transaction of his life.'[3] There, one feels, speaks Dr. Johnson, too, Jane Austen's favourite writer in prose.

'The basis of all excellence is truth', Dr. Johnson observed in his *Life of Cowley*, and he asserted elsewhere that it is necessary that individuals should be able to trust each other, even from the point of

---

[1] *Letters to His Son*, April 30, O.S. 1752.
[2] Chapter 51.   [3] Chapter 46.

view of convenience. Without mutual faith, society could hardly function, and the type of duplicity that Frank Churchill practises and Lord Chesterfield preaches makes any moral basis to society impossible. Their attitude to society is a polite and refined version of the Machiavellianism popular in England during the sixteenth and seventeenth centuries, though the idea that the end justifies the means is applied to personal relationships rather than to society as a whole.

The first volume of the novel concludes with this debate, and Emma's opinion that, for once, Mr. Knightley is being illiberal: 'to take a dislike to a young man, only because he appeared to be of a different disposition from himself, was unworthy the real liberality of mind which she was always used to acknowledge in him; for with all the high opinion of himself, which she had often laid to his charge, she had never before for a moment supposed it could make him unjust to the merit of another'. To be 'illiberal' is to have a coarseness of sentiment which is the equivalent in thought to the cliché or commonplace phrase in style or expression. Thus, in *Pride and Prejudice*, Lydia Bennet describes Mary King as 'a nasty little freckled thing', and Elizabeth 'was shocked to think that, however incapable of such coarseness of *expression* herself, the coarseness of the *sentiment* was little other than her own breast had formerly harboured and fancied liberal'.[1] Coarseness of expression in Jane Austen leads inevitably to breaches of conduct.

Mr. Knightley is also 'illiberal' at this point because he is intolerant, and tolerance is a virtue which is very highly regarded by Jane Austen, not because she believes in suffering fools gladly, but because she recognises that, in actual fact, the world is made up, to a large extent, of knaves and fools. She also distrusts the self-righteous person, and Mr. Knightley is obviously in danger of this failing. In *Sense and Sensibility*, Elinor expresses the more tolerant view, which is not inconsistent with a proper exercise of moral judgment: 'I will not raise objections against anyone's conduct on so *illiberal* a foundation, as a difference in judgment from myself, or a deviation from what I may think right and consistent.'[2] To be liberal is to be generous, and everybody is in need of generosity. In face of disagreements and disappointments, which are bound to occur, it means

[1] Chapter 39.   [2] Chapter 15.

being dignified, recognising that the other person may be right, and agreeing to differ. It involves refinement and delicacy in the exercise of judgment, and yet it implies intellectual strength and toughness. In *Pride and Prejudice*, Mrs. Bennet is described as having a 'weak understanding and illiberal mind'.[1] Darcy is described as being 'a liberal master', 'a liberal man, and did much good among the poor.' He has liberality and 'he had the means of exercising it'.[2] In *Mansfield Park* the meanness of Mrs. Norris is 'illiberal', Tom Bertram has 'all the liberal dispositions of an eldest son, who feels born only for expense and enjoyment',[3] while, on the other hand, Henry Crawford has 'the liberality and good-breeding of a gentleman'.[4] The virtue of liberality is an essential characteristic of a lady and a gentleman, according to Jane Austen. When Emma accuses Mr. Knightley of being 'illiberal', she is, therefore, implying that, for once, the perfect gentleman has failed to live up to the moral standards which, for the greater part of the novel, he personifies. Occasionally, as in the case of Tom Bertram, liberality can be associated with the idea of an epicurean self-indulgence. When Frank Churchill goes to London, apparently merely to have a hair-cut, 'liberal allowances were made for the little excesses of such a handsome young man'.[5] In this case, Mr. Knightley's greater severity, his independent disassociation from the weakly generous view of ordinary, commonplace society, is a proof of his integrity, which always included, for Jane Austen, a certain amount of nonconformity. She sympathised with the Evangelicals, though belonging to the Established Church.

2. *The Second Volume*

The second volume introduces Jane Fairfax, whose presence is to test Emma's 'liberality' as Frank Churchill tries that of Mr. Knightley, though Emma has known Jane since they were children. After frequent reading, one notices the technical skill of the indirect

[1] Chapter 42.   [2] Chapters 43, 44, 52.   [3] Chapter 2.
[4] Chapter 30.   [5] Chapter 25.

introduction of the character through the dialogue of Miss Bates, with whom Jane Fairfax, the personification of elegance, forms a complete contrast. In the second chapter the character is directly described and formally introduced. Two chapters later, 'the charming Augusta Hawkins,' who claims all the elegance that Jane Fairfax really possesses, is introduced and described, but her actual appearance, as the vulgar Mrs. Elton, is delayed until the fourteenth chapter of the volume (Chapter 32). In the one case the confused speech of Miss Bates underlines the distinguished reserve and refinement of the person whose character is then delicately outlined in the sensitively detached and impersonal prose of Jane Austen herself. The prose which introduces 'the charming Augusta Hawkins' is detached and impersonal, too, but sympathy for Harriet, Emma and the community as a whole is suggested by the acidic undertone and the jaunty rhythms. When the speech of Mrs. Elton finally bursts on Emma in all its insensitiveness and coarseness, its essential kinship with the illiteracy of the speech of Miss Bates is plain.

Jane Fairfax, though apparently the embodiment of virtue, has not been liked by most readers of *Emma*. She appears, for the greater part of the novel, to be a simple and direct presentation of virtue, especially of virtue as it is represented by fortitude and passive suffering. She resembles Fanny Price, the heroine of *Mansfield Park*, in this respect. Emma, with her greater complexity resulting from the mingling of good and evil in her nature, is also the more human character of the two. Jane Fairfax takes comparatively little direct part in the story. She exists mainly as a character about which other people talk and think, and it is difficult to interest oneself very much, except in so far as she appears through the consciousness of Emma, in particular. She is as cold and distant, so far as the reader is concerned, as she is for the heroine herself. The praise of Mr. Knightley is noted and registered as information giving her a theoretical superiority, but it is not until the intrigue is finally resolved that one appreciates that the negative Pharisaism of Jane Fairfax has been the mask concealing intense suffering and has represented the genuine triumph of charity.

The contrast between Jane Fairfax and Emma derives partly from the Richardsonian tradition in the novel which Jane Austen had out-

grown. One of the conventions of this type of novel was that there
should be a lively and quiet girl. Miss Howe and Clarissa, Clemen-
tina and Harriet Byron in *Sir Charles Grandison*, Indiana Lynmere
and Camilla Tyrold in Fanny Burney's *Camilla* follow this pattern,
and a similar contrast can be found in the conduct books, some, such
as those of Lord Halifax and Lord Chesterfield, recommending wit
and being considered immoral, while others, such as those of Mrs.
Chapone, Dr. Gregory and Thomas Gisborne preached stern
morality, and recommended the domestic virtues. Jane Austen's reaction to these two opposing ideals was ambiguous, though she had a
natural delight in wit. In her novels, Elinor and Marianne in *Sense
and Sensibility*, Jane and Elizabeth Bennet in *Pride and Prejudice*, Fanny
Price and Mary Crawford in *Mansfield Park*, provide a contrast between the quiet and the gay. In *Emma*, Jane Austen is much more
concerned than in her previous novels with presenting a detailed
study of the heroine, through whose eyes a large part of the action
and our impressions of the other characters are seen. The introduction
of the Richardsonian pattern a third of the way through the novel
disturbs the delicate balance of comparisons and contrasts that has
been established, and results in a character who never comes to life
being inserted into the story. It is true that Jane Fairfax is counter-
balanced by Frank Churchill, and that her presence enables Jane
Austen to round off the story neatly with their marriage. But as a
representative of virtue she never establishes the vital, dramatic relationship with the heroine that justifies the introduction of Frank
Churchill, and as a self-righteous contrast to the naughtiness of Emma
and Frank Churchill, she only succeeds in making virtue, itself, appear
unconvincing and unreal. One's sympathy is aroused, however, by
the contrast between her accomplishments and the lack of intelligence
of the company she has to keep. As a victim, a potential Fanny Price,
she is convincing. Obviously, this exploitation and degradation of
the sensitive and intelligent by ordinary, mediocre society represented an important element in life, as Jane Austen knew and experienced it. In this respect, there is a similarity between Jane Fairfax
and Emma, though the latter does not have the apparent threat of
poverty to intimidate her, or the final humiliation of the patronage of
Mrs. Elton.

If Jane Fairfax's reserve and coldness are repulsive to Emma, she shows that these characteristics are to be preferred to those of the more pliant and sociable qualities of the simple Harriet, 'so easily pleased',[1] who resembles so closely the aunt, Miss Bates, whose company the elegant Jane has to endure, 'so silly—so satisfied—so smiling.'[2] Emma's delight in controlling the lives of others encourages her to prefer the company of those who are more easily controlled, and leads to a fatal mistake in discrimination. 'The charming Augusta Hawkins', to whom one is introduced, had also been 'so easily impressed' by Mr. Elton,[3] and is to inflict herself on both Emma and Jane. However little in common Emma and Mr. Elton have, they both take the line of least resistance. Augusta Hawkins as a substitute for Emma, as a wife, is hardly more absurd than Harriet as a substitute for Jane, as a friend, and Mr. Elton at least has the excuse that the choice of the superior person is first made, and refused. He falls from the sublime to the ridiculous, whereas Emma, with freedom of choice, prefers the simple girl who is essentially adolescent to the cultivated young woman whose company would have provided a challenge to her own immaturity. Jane Fairfax, who becomes involved in the 'governess-trade', is qualified as an educator, whereas Emma only thinks that she is.

When Jane Austen attempts to define the qualities that make up an ideal character, one sees how close her drama of personal relationships is to the Johnsonian moral essay. Jane Fairfax had been given an excellent education, 'living constantly with right-minded and well-informed people, her heart and understanding had received every advantage of discipline and culture'.[4] Dr. Johnson and Jane Austen could assume that their readers would understand what was meant by discipline and culture, and why they should be connected with each other. Their own work was the result of the same discipline, diligence and almost obstinate perseverance. Something of the mixture of *élan* and organising ability needed in a successful military operation is shown in the technique of creation of these two writers. Their artistic standards are almost ascetic in their severity, and the moral standards which their writings embody are equally severe. Yet, they

[1] Chapter 21.   [2] Chapter 10.
[3] Chapter 22.   [4] Chapter 20.

both enjoyed life, and could appreciate a Boswell or a Frank Churchill
as well as a Sir Joshua Reynolds or a Mr. Knightley. Jane Fairfax,
despite her superior education and elegance, is not perfect. Her
faults, though fewer, are more serious than those of the far from faultless heroine. Mr. Knightley considers that 'she has not the open
temper which a man would wish for in a wife . . . her sensibilities,
I suspect, are strong—and her temper excellent in its power of forbearance, patience, self-control; but it wants openness. She is reserved, more reserved, I think, than she used to be—And I love an
open temper'.[1] Elegance of person and of mind, grace, 'a style of
beauty' and distinction are all granted, and contrast favourably with
the vulgarity of her surroundings, but the very generosity which is
partly the cause of Emma's faults also confirms her superiority.

The fourth chapter of this volume, introducing and describing
Augusta Hawkins, is followed by Emma's meeting with Frank
Churchill. His visit coincides with the end of winter, even Harriet
has 'a look of spring', and, for Emma, 'the worn-out past was sunk
in the freshness of what was coming'. He has spirit and liveliness
himself like the season, and his arrival is the cause of 'a most delight-
ful re-animation of exhausted spirits'. Unlike Mrs. Elton, it seems
that he is going to be a real addition to society: 'a *very* good looking
young man; height, air, address, all were unexceptionable . . . he
looked quick and sensible. She felt immediately that she should like
him; and there was a well-bred ease of manner, and a readiness to
talk, which convinced her that he came intending to be acquainted
with her, and that acquainted they soon must be'.[2] Frank Churchill
has a certain enthusiasm and eagerness in his nature which appeal to
Emma, who resembles him in this respect. This characteristic may
and does, sometimes, result in vulgarity, but it is regarded by Jane
Austen, in this novel, as more attractive and superior morally to too
much reserve or caution. It is connected with the gift that both of
them have of enjoying life and giving pleasure to others. Frank
knows how to make himself agreeable, even if it involves lying. His
gallantry contrasts with the forced and clumsy attempts of the un-
lucky Mr. Elton. His compliments are much more delicate and tact-
ful, and, therefore, acceptable. Instead of forcing his company on

[1] Chapter 33.   [2] Chapter 23.

Emma, or exploiting the fact that everyone expects them to be attracted to each other, he goes off to see Jane Fairfax, with whom, as he says 'there was that degree of acquaintance at Weymouth which—,' when his father interrupts.[1] This appears to be merely another example of social tact, though there is a motive for Frank Churchill's words and actions which is only made clear at the end of the story. When he goes to the village shop, Ford's, for some gloves, 'the sleek, well-tied parcels of "Men's Beavers" and "York Tan"' are described.[2] It is a danger signal: there is something rather too sleek about Frank Churchill himself, compared with the simple eagerness and elegance of Emma. While the gloves are being bought, Emma repeats her enquiry about the friendship with Jane Fairfax at Weymouth, and the discretion of Frank Churchill's reply is rather glib, deft and sleek, too. The following day he goes off to London, apparently with the sole purpose of having his hair cut.

Frank Churchill inherits his father's sociable nature. Just as Mr. Weston has been criticised by Mr. John Knightley for what he regards as a weakness of character, so the thoughtful Mr. Knightley contrasts with his rival. The difference is partly that between youth and middle age, or, to continue the analogy of the seasons, between spring and summer, but it is also the difference between a view of life that stresses the importance of traditional values and an individualism which side-tracks or ignores moral issues, stresses the importance of maintaining a surface appearance of good manners, and allows freedom from the restraints of custom. The different types of pride, and the proper kind of pride for the individual to show, are further issues raised in the implied contrast between Frank Churchill and Mr. Knightley.

When Frank Churchill takes his first walk around Highbury with Emma, he talks enthusiastically about dancing: 'Emma was rather surprised to see the constitution of the Westons prevail so decidedly against the habits of the Churchills. He seemed to have all the life and spirit, cheerful feelings, and social inclinations of his father, and nothing of the pride or reserve of Enscombe. Of pride, indeed, there was, perhaps, scarcely enough; his indifference to a confusion of

[1] Chapter 23.   [2] Chapter 24.

rank, bordered too much on inelegance of mind.'[1] On the one hand, pride is opposed to sociability, and connected with the reserve of the wealthy Churchills. Yet there is a proper pride, based upon rank, the kind that Mr. Knightley has. Frank Churchill, with his friendliness and lack of discrimination, is in danger of lapsing into the vulgarity of Mr. Elton. Even in *Pride and Prejudice*, where the pride of Darcy is eventually humbled, Charlotte Lucas maintains that he has an excuse and a right to be proud.[2] Darcy, himself, remarks that 'vanity is a weakness indeed. But pride—where there is a real superiority of mind, pride will be always under good regulation'.[3]

Jane Austen appears to have admired pride as a moral virtue and the natural expression of nobility of character, but to have disapproved of it when it was the result of haughtiness produced merely by wealth and rank. In *Pride and Prejudice*, Mr. Bingley's sisters are merely 'proud and conceited'[4]; Miss Churchill's brother and his wife were 'full of pride and importance'[5]; Emma, who is herself a snob, remarks to Harriet, who has just mentioned Miss Nashe's sister who married a linen-draper, 'one should be sorry to see greater pride or refinement in the teacher of a school'.[6] Bingley's sisters, together with Miss Churchill's brother and his wife, can be left to their fate, but Emma is still capable of redemption and her mistake is the result of her generally false estimate of mere rank and wealth. In *Persuasion*, on the other hand, the heroine Anne Elliot wishes that her father and sister had more pride, and says 'I certainly am proud, too proud to enjoy a welcome which depends so entirely upon place'.[7] This is a proper kind of pride, completely the opposite of snobbery, and reflects the greater intelligence and detachment of Anne. Even Mr. Weston is more sensible on the theme of pride than Emma, as his ironic description of the Churchills shows: 'Mr. Churchill has pride; but his pride is nothing to his wife's: his is a quiet, indolent, gentleman-like sort of pride that would harm nobody, and only make himself a little helpless and tiresome; but her pride is arrogance and insolence! And what inclines one less to bear, she has

---

[1] *Emma*, Chapter 24.   [2] *Pride and Prejudice*, Chapter 5.
[3] *Ibid*., Chapter 11.   [4] *Ibid*., Chapter 4.
[5] *Emma*, Chapter 2.   [6] *Ibid*., Chapter 7.
[7] *Persuasion*, Chapter 16.

no pretence of family or blood. She was nobody when he married her, barely the daughter of a gentleman; and ever since her being turned into a Churchill she has out-Churchill'd them all in high and mighty claims: but in herself, I asure you, she is an upstart.'[1] Whatever criticisms of pride Mr. Weston may make, one notes that he retains the traditional respect for 'family' and 'blood'. On the other hand, Mr. Woodhouse considers that Frank Churchill 'is not quite the thing',[2] and though his reasons for thinking and saying so are trivial, and one does not have much sympathy with his peevish complaints, which are primarily intended to be comical, there is a sense in which the remark is just, and represents the instinctive resistance of the older generation to the lack of manners of the young. Frank Churchill does not always show such tactlessness: 'Some of the objects of his curiosity spoke very amiable feelings. He begged to be shewn the house which his father had lived in so long, and which had been the home of his father's father; and on recollecting that an old woman who had nursed him was still living, walked in quest of her cottage from one end of the street to the other.'[3] It is in such glimpses that Jane Austen suggests the background of the traditional, provincial society, whose existence and permanency she takes for granted.

The occasional deviation from what she regards as normal in society fascinates Jane Austen. The Coles are representatives of the 'new rich', intruders like the Eltons into the delicately graded hierarchy of the rural order, but the Eltons remain essentially 'outsiders', while society 'adjusts' itself to meet the demands of the Coles. 'The Coles had been settled some years in Highbury, and were very good sort of people—friendly, liberal, and unpretending; but, on the other hand, they were of low origin, in trade, and only moderately genteel. On their first coming into the country, they had lived in proportion to their income, quietly, keeping little company, and that little unexpensively; but the last year or two had brought them a considerable increase of means—the house in town had yielded greater profits, and fortune in general had smiled on them. With their wealth, their views increased; their want of a larger house, their inclination for more company. They added to their house, to their

[1] *Emma*, Chapter 36.   [2] *Ibid.*, Chapter 29.   [3] *Ibid*, Chapter 24.

number of servants, to their expenses of every sort; and by this time
were, in fortune and style of living, second only to the family at
Hartfield. Their love of society, and their new dining-room, prepared
every body for their keeping dinner-company; and a few parties,
chiefly among the single men, had already taken place. The regular
and best families Emma could hardly suppose they would presume
to invite—neither Donwell, nor Hartfield, nor Randalls. Nothing
should tempt *her* to go, if they did; and she regretted that her father's
known habits would be giving her refusal less meaning than she could
wish. The Coles were very respectable in their way, but they ought to
be taught that it was not for them to arrange the terms on which the
superior families would visit them. This lesson, she very much
feared, they would receive only from herself; she had little hope of
Mr. Knightley, none of Mr. Weston.'[1] The ambiguous way in
which such a description fluctuates between an apparently impersonal
statement of fact, and Emma's prejudiced and snobbish reaction,
leaves one slightly uncertain about the attitude that one is supposed to
take towards the Coles. Donwell and Randalls do receive an invita-
tion, and when Emma is invited too, she is easily persuaded to accept.
Mr. Weston describes them as 'friendly, good sort of people as ever
lived, and who have been your neighbours these *ten* years'.[2] Yet
Emma recalls, just before she goes to the party, that 'among the failings of Mr. Elton, even in the days of his favour, none had disturbed
her more than his propensity to dine with Mr. Cole.'[3] After the
visit, she 'did not repent her condescension in going to the Coles . . .
worthy people, who deserved to be made happy!'[4]

The most common test of endurance to which the heroine in Jane
Austen's novels has to submit is the accepting of the world as she
finds it, the strain involved in living in inferior company. There can
be no doubt that the Coles, however worthy, represent a level of
mediocrity to which it is only too easy to sink. Their party provides
the appropriate background for the trivialities of the conversation of
Emma and Frank Churchill. The heroine, herself, notes how 'The
children came in, and were talked to and admired amid the usual rate
of conversation; a few clever things said, a few downright silly, but

[1] Chapter 25.   [2] *Emma*, Chapter 25.
[3] *Ibid.*, Chapter 26.   [4] *Ibid.*, Chapter 27.

by much the larger proportion neither the one nor the other—nothing worse than everyday remarks, dull repetitions, old news, and heavy jokes.'[1]

This question of speech is not so simple as might appear. It is partly used as a means of estimating degrees of intelligence, but it does not provide an absolute standard of either intelligence or integrity. The subject of conversational powers is itself touched with irony. It is connected with the habits of gossip and small-talk, and an over-indulgence in it leads to inaccuracy and slackness of language. On the other hand, to introduce intelligent conversation is a sign of good-breeding. The ideal seems to consist in striking a proper balance between talking too much, and being too silent. Glibness and facility are distrusted, particularly in men. Frank Churchill is a great talker, while Mr. Knightley, even when proposing, says that he cannot make speeches; 'If I loved you less, I might be able to talk about it more.'[2] Mrs. Weston thinks that Mr. Knightley would not be much disturbed by Miss Bates. Little things do not irritate him: 'She might talk on; and if he wanted to say anything himself, he would only talk louder, and drown her voice"[3] Great conversationalists are usually insincere as well as incorrect in their use of language, and reading a novel of Jane Austen is largely a matter of distinguishing between the nuances and gradations of insincerity in 'the usual rate of conversation'. The importance of conversation makes the novels naturally dramatic, and they foreshadow later examples of satirical comedy in fiction, implying a civilised standard of personal relationships. Perhaps it was the drama which made Jane Austen appreciate the way in which the presence of a character can be conveyed by the negative means of absence and silence, as well as the effect caused by the delayed or gradual introduction of a character.

There is always a danger that, in repeating the conversation of dull, limited people, such as Mr. Woodhouse and Miss Bates, the novel itself will become dull. Sir Walter Scott had pointed out this possible flaw in *The Quarterly Review*.[4] The skill of the novelist is in the total

[1] *Emma*, Chapter 26.   [2] *Ibid.*, Chapter 49.   [3] *Ibid.*, Chapter 26.

[4] His comments still provide an excellent critical introduction, at an elementary level, but *The Quarterly Review*, No. XXVII, is not generally available.

pattern of the dialogue, the mingling of the lively and intelligent with the commonplace and stupid. Jane Austen excels in showing the complications that exist beneath the simplest character or situation. Mr. Knightley 'does nothing mysteriously',[1] and yet he is just as complex as Frank Churchill, who delights in mystery. He is not representative of abstract virtue, like the Sir Charles Grandison of Richardson, but a human, even prosaic and completely convincing person. Emma appears to be much more subtle than Mr. Knightley, and yet she can still take a simple delight in the ordinary routine of provincial life. She shares with Jane Austen herself the ability to see the artistic wealth which exists in the obvious and humdrum situation, or character. That is one reason why Harriet attracts her, but Harriet is merely one example of the resources possible for the imaginative, observing mind, in the most unpropitious material.

A typical example of imaginative observation by the heroine occurs in a scene where she and Harriet have gone to Ford's to shop. 'Harriet, tempted by every thing and swayed by half a word, was always very long at a purchase; and while she was still hanging over muslins and changing her mind, Emma went to the door for amusement,—Much could not be hoped from the traffic of even the busiest part of Highbury; Mr. Perry walking hastily by, Mr. William Cox letting himself in at the office door, Mr. Cole's carriage horses returning from exercise, or a stray letter-boy on an obstinate mule, were the liveliest objects she could presume to expect; and when her eyes fell only on the butcher with his tray, a tidy old woman travelling homewards from shop with her full basket, two curs quarrelling over a dirty bone, and a string of dawdling children round the baker's little bow-window eyeing the gingerbread, she knew she had no reason to complain, and was amused enough; quite enough still to stand at the door. A mind lively and at ease, can do with seeing nothing, and can see nothing that does not answer.'[2] The comment that *Emma* 'shows Fielding's characteristic strength in conveying the sense of society as a whole . . .'[3] would be justified to a greater extent than it is if these characters and scenes were developed. It is only a glimpse, however. There is a similar one in *Persuasion*: 'When Lady

---

[1] *Emma*, Chapter 26.   [2] *Ibid.*, Chapter 27.
[3] Ian Watt, *The Rise of the Novel*, p. 297.

Russell, not long afterwards, was entering Bath on a wet afternoon, and driving through the long course of streets from the Old Bridge to Camden-place, amidst the dash of other carriages, the heavy rumble of carts and drays, the bawling of newsmen, muffin-men and milk-men, and the ceaseless clink of pattens, she made no complaint. No, these were noises which belonged to the winter pleasures. . . .'[1]

The world that Emma and Lady Russell observe is not the world of the Jane Austen novel, but of ordinary life below the level even of the commonplace characters who are only slightly sketched in the stories. It is the world that George Eliot was to include, but Jane Austen selected and deliberately limited herself, ignoring the parts of society that did not interest her. George Eliot would agree with her that one's fellow-mortals must be accepted as they are, with elements of nobility in the meanest, and a terrifying capacity for self-betrayal in the finest. There is more compassion in the Victorian novelist than in the ruthlessly unsentimental Jane Austen, though it would be a mistake to consider that the defender of Miss Bates and, even, of Harriet Smith, or the observer of the threatened fate of Jane Fairfax, is completely lacking in compassion. Both writers were concerned with the search for truth, and were equally aware how difficult it is to disentangle truth from falsehood. It was for the quality of truthfulness that George Eliot admired Dutch paintings, 'these faithful pictures of a monotonous homely existence'.[2] She refers directly to 'the ease we felt in those scenes where we were born' and describes how shallow life would be 'if the loves and sanctities of our life had no deep immovable roots in memory'.[3] Jane Austen implies such things: they are inferred, rather than stated. Both writers are concerned with what George Eliot calls 'the primitive fellowship of kindred',[4] but Jane Austen is able to take it for granted, while George Eliot, however much she reveres the family, is much more aware of elements of revolt against its authority, in society as a whole.

It may be said of Emma, as George Eliot remarks of Dorothea, the

---

[1] *Persuasion*, Chapter 14.
[2] *Adam Bede*, Book II, Chapter 17.
[3] *The Mill on the Floss*, Book II, Chapter 1.
[4] *Ibid.*, Book II, Chapter 2.

heroine of *Middlemarch*, that 'permanent rebellion, the disorder of a life without some loving reverent resolve, was not possible to her'.[1] George Eliot, however, is describing her heroine's frustration six weeks after her wedding. The conventional 'perfect happiness of the union', with which *Emma* concludes, clearly marks the point where Jane Austen considers that it would be immodest and unnecessary to consider further. This is a limitation, and some readers have questioned whether Emma and Mr. Knightley would have enjoyed such a quiet, conventional marriage. Certainly, with Dorothea and Casaubon, George Eliot explores the problem of the incompatible marriage in a way that Jane Austen does not attempt to do. When she touches on the problem, as in the relationship of Mr. and Mrs. Bennet in *Pride and Prejudice*, it is regarded as a subject to provide comedy, and is dealt with in an almost burlesque manner. In *Emma*, mature married life, as represented by the Westons, Mr. and Mrs. John Knightley and the Eltons, is a subject of comparatively minor mportance, while it is the main theme of *Middlemarch*. Jane Austen is interested in the problems that arise during the passing of the heroine from adolescence to maturity. One can see her influence on George Eliot in *Daniel Deronda*, but, again, the scope of the later novelist is wider, and the psychology more complex and subtle.

'You have the art of giving pictures in a few words', Frank Churchill says to Emma,[2] and this is the art in which Jane Austen is more consistently successful than George Eliot. The economy of means used to achieve her intentions and artistic effects is exemplary. George Eliot, whose style can be infinitely flexible and sensitive, is sometimes extremely clumsy. As Virginia Woolf has observed, 'it is partly that her hold upon dialogue, when it is not dialect, is slack; and partly that she seems to shrink with an elderly dread of fatigue from the effort of emotional concentration. She allows her heroines to talk too much. She has little verbal felicity. She lacks the unerring taste which chooses one sentence and compresses the heart of the scene within that. "Whom are you going to dance with?" asked Mr. Knightley, at the Westons' ball. "With you, if you will ask me," said Emma; and she has said enough. Mrs. Casaubon would

[1] *Middlemarch*, Book II, Chapter XX.
[2] *Emma*, Chapter 29.

have talked for an hour and we should have looked out of the window'.[1]

Jane Austen combines a gift for selecting significant detail with an ability to show the changes and slow, complex development of relationships. Emma and Mr. Knightley are old friends, and there is all the stability and depth of a long acquaintance to counteract any temporary disagreement. Between the heroine and Frank Churchill one sees the change and development of an unstable relationship which is built up rapidly and then collapses. Frank Churchill first seriously impinges on Emma's consciousness just as she is beginning to try to forget about Mr. Elton.[2] From this point she becomes increasingly interested in him, and the crucial point in her response is communicated in a descriptive soliloquy in Chapter 31. The thirtieth chapter describes Emma's joyful anticipations of a ball, about which Mr. Knightley is provokingly indifferent. 'Fine dancing, I believe, like virtue, must be its own reward', he remarks. Frank Churchill is then recalled by Mrs. Churchill, the ball cancelled, and he takes leave of Emma with what she believes to be regret and disappointment for the loss of her company. She prepares to sink back into the commonplace, humdrum existence at Hartfield. Before doing so, she examines her feelings: 'This sensation of listlessness, weariness, stupidity, this disinclination to sit down and employ myself, this feeling of every thing's being dull and insipid about the house! I must be in love; I should be the oddest creature in the world if I were not—for a few weeks at least. Well! evil to some is always good to others. I shall have many fellow-mourners for the ball, if not for Frank Churchill, but Mr. Knightley will be happy. He may spend the evening with his dear William Larkins now if he likes.'[3]

This passage does not merely describe Emma's emotional state, it provides the reader with insight into the degree of her self-awareness. Jane Austen reveals through the very rhythms of speech and thought the unconscious and hidden thoughts and feelings of her characters. How far is Emma's listlessness merely due to boredom with Hartfield, and with her father, in particular, and to what extent is it due to

[1] 'George Eliot', *The Common Reader, First Series*, uniform edition, p. 216.

[2] *Emma*, Chapter 14.   [3] Chapter 30.

chagrin at Frank's departure? Is she deceiving herself when she thinks she may be in love? The phrase 'I should be the oddest creature in the world if I were not', suggests a curious detachment, which is emphasised by the light-hearted after-thought, 'for a few weeks at least'. Emma is laughing at herself as well as analysing her feelings, and the fact that she can question and doubt in this way implies that her emotions are not overpowering. The jealousy she betrays over Mr. Knightley's preference of the company of William Larkins to her own has to be taken into account when she questions herself about her relationship with Frank Churchill. Mr. Knightley's cheerful look is equally a betrayal of his feelings, while, with a final ironic twist, the person who is suffering most, Jane Fairfax, appears to Emma to be merely acting with an odious composure and indifference, for which she is excused, because she has a headache.

The next chapter continues and develops Emma's self-analysis. The heroine is too sensible and intelligent to indulge in self-deception, at this point, either about herself or about Frank Churchill: 'though thinking of him so much, and, as she sat drawing or working, forming a thousand amusing schemes for the progress and close of their attachment, fancying interesting dialogues, and inventing elegant letters; the conclusion of every imaginary declaration on his side was that she *refused him*. Their affection was always to subside into friendship. Every thing tender and charming was to mark their parting; but still they were to part. When she became sensible of this, it struck her that she could not be very much in love; for in spite of her previous and fixed determination never to quit her father, never to marry, a strong attachment certainly must produce more of a struggle than she could foresee in her own feelings.

'I do not find myself making any use of the word *sacrifice*,' said she.—'In not one of all my clever replies, my delicate negatives, is there any allusion to making a sacrifice. I do suspect that he is not really necessary to my happiness. So much the better. I certainly will not persuade myself to feel more than I do. I am quite enough in love. I should be sorry to be more.'[1] The soliloquy marks the end of the relationship in its more serious aspect, and the episode has been concentrated into a space equivalent to about a half of one of the three

[1] Chapter 31.

volumes into which the novel was originally divided. The reluctance to leave her father, which Emma expresses here, is to provide the final stumbling-block at the end of the novel to the consummation of her relationship with Mr. Knightley.

The last five chapters of the second volume are dominated by Mrs. Elton. After being mentioned and described in the fourth chapter, she appears at just the right moment to add variety to the story and with a special kind of delayed-action effect in the fourteenth chapter of the volume. The lady whom Mr. Elton eventually marries, 'the charming Augusta Hawkins', is far from fastidious. The speed of his courtship, after he has been rejected by Emma, is only equalled by the ease of the capture. Augusta Hawkins 'was in possession of an independent fortune, of so many thousands as would always be called ten . . . the history which he had to give Mrs. Cole of the rise and progress of the affair was so glorious—the steps so quick, from the accidental rencontre, to the dinner at Mrs. Green's, and the party at Mrs. Brown's—smiles and blushes rising in importance—with consciousness and agitation richly scattered—the lady had been so easily impressed—so sweetly disposed—had in short, to use a most intelligible phrase, been so ready to have him, that vanity and prudence were equally contented'.[1] The lady who had been so easily impressed by Mr. Elton is to regard herself as Emma's equal, to discover that 'Knightley', as she calls him, is a gentleman, that Mrs. Weston has good manners, and to describe Mr. Woodhouse as an 'old beau'. The ease of manner of Mrs. Elton represents the lack of tradition of the 'new rich', commercial class from the town, and is intended to contrast with the traditional good taste of the rural, provincial order, betrayed by the worldly vicar. Emma's first impression is that Mrs. Elton has 'ease' but not elegance, as opposed to Jane Fairfax, the perfect example of feminine elegance, whom Mrs. Elton is later to patronise. 'For a young woman, a stranger, a bride, there was too much ease.'[2] The reference to her 'easy conceit' is an example of the way in which Jane Austen connects social and moral flaws. Mrs. Elton, herself, affects to despise 'modern ease', which she opposes to Mr. Woodhouse's 'quaint old-fashioned politeness'.[3] When she refers familiarly to 'Jane', Frank Churchill is critical and comments on her 'easy'

[1] Chapter 22.   [2] Chapter 32.   [3] Chapter 35.

manners: '"Jane!"—repeated Frank Churchill, with a look of surprise and displeasure.—"That is easy—but Miss Fairfax does not disapprove it, I suppose." '[1]

Once Emma meets Mrs. Elton it does not take her long to arrive at an opinion of her worth: 'the quarter of an hour quite convinced her that Mrs. Elton was a vain woman, extremely well satisfied with herself, and thinking much of her own importance; that she meant to shine and be very superior, but with manners which had been formed in a bad school, pert and familiar; that all her notions were drawn from one set of people, and one style of living; that if not foolish she was ignorant, and that her society would certainly do Mr. Elton no good'.[2] Mrs. Elton is a 'static' character like Miss Bates, Mr. John Knightley, Mr. Martin, Mr. and Mrs. Weston, and Mr. Woodhouse. Though their actual personalities do not change, the attitudes and reactions of the other main characters do, or one finds out more about them, as in the case of Jane Fairfax and Frank Churchill, so that one's whole opinion of them is changed. The distinction between the 'static' and 'dynamic' characters can be further developed. Mrs. Elton, Miss Bates and Mr. Woodhouse are essentially caricatures, with fixed mannerisms and a limited number of qualities, on which they depend for the comic effect that they produce. Whereas Miss Bates is wholly comic, a conventional type of character deriving from Miss Larolles in Fanny Burney's *Cecilia*, Mr. Woodhouse is partly to be admired for his courtesy and manners, and partly to be feared for the frustrating, deadening effect he has on the life of the heroine. Mrs. Elton is partly a figure of fun, with her references to Maple Grove, the barouche-landau, her 'caro sposo' (a phrase used by a Lady Honoria in Fanny Burney's *Cecilia*)[3] and 'Hymen's saffron robe'. When she tries to dominate the society into which she has entered, and attempts to patronise and exploit Jane Fairfax, she reveals the evil which lies beneath her absurdity. Mr. Woodhouse can mention 'a matter of mere common politeness and good-breeding' as a thing to be taken for granted: Mrs. Elton does not know of their existence: 'self-important, presuming, familiar, ignorant, and ill-bred. She had a little beauty and a little accomplishment, but so little judgment that she thought herself coming with superior knowledge of the world, to enliven and

[1] Chapter 38.   [2] Chapter 32.   [3] *Cecilia*, Book VI, Chapter 2.

improve a country neighbourhood; and conceived Miss Hawkins to have held such a place in society as Mrs. Elton's consequence only could surpass'.[1] Emma's imagination and snobbery suggest to her, at one point, that a friend of Mrs. Elton is 'probably some vulgar dashing widow, who, with the help of a boarder, just made a shift to live!'[2] However critical Jane Austen may be of her heroine, one is meant, in this case, to identify oneself with her judgment and point of view. Mrs. Elton reminds one of the 'bold, swaggering ladies' called 'rattles' whom Swift describes in his *Letter to a Very Young Lady on Her Marriage*. There is a Swiftian ruthlessness about Jane Austen's treatment of Mrs. Elton, which is lacking in her ridicule of Miss Bates, who is merely a harmless gossip. The comedy of the one character conceals a hatred which is never far below the surface, while the unconscious humour of the other is relished with a pitying acceptance of the boredom which it involves that only occasionally breaks out into open contempt.

3. The Third Volume

The third volume begins with Emma's reflections on the state of her feelings towards Frank Churchill: 'her own attachment had really subsided into a mere nothing'. She thinks that he had always been the more in love of the two, a characteristic self-deception, but when they meet 'it was a clear thing he was less in love than he had been'. He is now mainly of interest to her as an alternative to Mr. Elton as the future husband of Harriet. It is the rescuing of Harriet from the gipsies that fires the imagination which is Emma's greatest gift.

The pleasures of the imagination had been discussed by Addison in *The Spectator*, Nos. 411-421 and by Akenside in poetry, as well as by Dr. Johnson, who remarked in his tale *Rasselas* that 'there is no man whose imagination does not sometimes predominate over his reason, who can regulate his attention wholly by his will, and whose ideas will come and go at his command'.[3] Jane Austen shares the

[1] Chapter 33. [2] Chapter 32. [3] *Rasselas*, Chapter 44.

D

Johnsonian hostility to imagination, 'that hunger of imagination, which preys incessantly upon life, and must be always appeased by some employment. Those who have already all that they can enjoy must enlarge their desires'.[1] That is the central theme of *Emma*, and the heroine's reactions to the incident between Harriet, Frank Churchill and the gipsies are typical of her imagination: 'Could a linguist, could a grammarian, could even a mathematician have seen what she did, have witnessed their appearance together, and heard their history of it, without feeling that circumstances had been at work to make them peculiarly interesting to each other? How much more must an imaginist, like herself, be on fire with speculation and foresight!—especially with such a ground of anticipation as her mind had already made.'[2]

After she has been involved in the self-deceptions that result from an over-indulgence in imagination, Emma accepts the suffering and disillusionment that the pursuit of truth inevitably causes. It is Mr. Knightley, the voice of reason, who triumphs in the end, and in the marriage between them Jane Austen resolves symbolically the conflict that had been discussed in the eighteenth century and with which the romantics were also concerned. Reason, in the eighteenth century, Johnsonian sense, personified by Mr. Knightley, enables one to see the facts, and find out the truth, but, however many mistakes she makes, the heroine, with her guesses, and imagination sometimes comes nearer to a full appreciation of the complexity of experience. Emma is not so sure that she is always right. Her scepticism and self-distrust, which are partly characteristic of adolescence, are also typical of Jane Austen herself. Mr. Knightley is partly blinded by prejudice and jealousy in his judgment of Frank Churchill, though he first suspects and detects the truth about Jane Fairfax and Frank Churchill.[3] When he asks Emma if she has not thought that Frank Churchill was an admirer of Jane Fairfax, she replies 'never'. Mr. Knightley arrives at his conclusion, however, by using imagination, Emma's special gift, in addition to his reason. He says that he has lately 'imagined' that he saw symptoms of attachment between them, and Emma remarks that he is allowing his imagination to wander. She proceeds to check his first 'essay' in imagination.

[1] *Rasselas*, Chapter 32.   [2] *Emma*, Chapter 39.   [3] Chapter 41.

When Frank Churchill went to London to arrange for the piano to be sent to Jane Fairfax, Mr. Knightley considered that he was trifling and silly,[1] while Emma observes more wisely and accurately that 'I do not know whether it ought to be so, but certainly silly things do cease to be silly if they are done by sensible people in an impudent way. Wickedness is always wickedness, but folly is not always folly. It depends upon the character of those who handle it. Mr. Knightley, he is *not* a trifling, silly young man.'[2] Frank Churchill finally asks her if she did not suspect the existence of the relationship, and she repeats the denial, but she is now bored by the subject of the intrigue, and is guilty of a slight untruth. She has forgotten (or Jane Austen has!) Mr. Knightley's suspicion and warning. Perhaps Emma would agree with Mary Crawford in *Mansfield Park* that '*Never* is a black word. But yes, in the *never* of conversation which means *not very often*, I do think it!': to which Edmund Bertram replies, 'The *nothing* of conversation has its gradations, I hope, as well as the *never*.'[3] Jane Austen's final comment on the nature of truth, the difficulty of the Johnsonian quest, occurs near the end of *Emma*, after the hero and heroine have been reconciled with each other: 'Seldom, very seldom, does complete truth belong to any human disclosure; seldom can it happen that something is not a little disguised, or a little mistaken; but where, as in this case, though the conduct is mistaken, the feelings are not, it may not be very material. Mr. Knightley could not impute to Emma a more relenting heart than she possessed, or a heart more disposed to accept of his.'[4]

The disingenuousness and double-dealing, the mixture of gallantry and trick that Mr. Knightley suspects in the 'word-making' with the box of letters[5] are correctly ascribed by him to Frank Churchill, who is, at the moment, a 'gallant young man, who seemed to love without feeling, and to recommend himself without complaisance'. The phrase 'sedate civility' used to describe Frank Churchill's manners is a good example of Jane Austen's command of nuance, which is the means by which she differentiates her characters, giving them light, shade and depth. The 'civility' of Frank Churchill contrasts with the true courtesy, delicacy and considerateness of Mr. Knightley

[1] Chapter 25.   [2] Chapter 26.   [3] *Mansfield Park*, Chapter 9.
[4] *Emma*, Chapter 49.   [5] *Ibid.*, Chapter 41.

which are consummately manifested in the party he gives at Donwell Abbey.

Jane Austen has an acute appreciation of the atmosphere or mood connected with different places, and she sometimes uses the contrast provided by two localities with an almost symbolic effect. The party at Donwell is followed on the next day by the trip to Box Hill, and the climax in the relations between the three main characters occurs during this brief, concentrated period. There are equivalents to Donwell Abbey in the other novels. Delaford, as described by Mrs. Jennings,[1] Cleveland which Elinor and Marianne visit,[2] Pemberley, the sight of which Elizabeth Bennet playfully suggests persuaded her to accept Darcy,[3] Mansfield Park where poor little Fanny Price grows to maturity, are superior places, providing the background to a more refined way of living, the civilised life of the English country house, which had been for centuries such an important influence on English culture. This way of life is traditional, and shows rural and provincial life at its best. There, ideally, the beautiful and the useful are perfectly combined. Jane Austen sees Donwell and the Abbey-Mill Farm, with the 'sweet view—sweet to the eye and the mind. English verdure, English culture, English comfort, seen under a sun bright, without being oppressive',[4] almost as a Garden of Eden, set in 'England's green and pleasant land.' Yet, it is an actual place, a scene which would have been appreciated by Cobbett during his rural rides, as well as by a poet.

The civilised decorum of the scene where Emma is shown some views of St. Mark's Place, Venice, which Mr. Knightley has provided for the entertainment of Mr. Woodhouse, contrasts with Mrs. Elton's enthusiasm for strawberry-picking, the hurried entrance and exit of Jane Fairfax, and the sudden appearance of Frank Churchill, hot and bad-tempered from his ride. Italy was associated in Jane Austen's mind with the harmony and grace of music, the romance as well as the horror and terror of the world of Ann Radliffe's novels. Harriet Smith hates Italian singing, because 'there is no understanding

---

[1] *Sense and Sensibility*, Chapter 30.   [2] *Ibid.*, Chapter 42.

[3] *Pride and Prejudice*, Chapter 43, the first chapter of the third and last volume.

[4] *Emma*, Chapter 42.

a word of it',[1] but in *Persuasion* the heroine, Anne Elliot translates at sight the lines of an Italian song.[2] Frank Churchill's conversation on his arrival at Donwell strikes a false note in every possible way, and his behaviour results in the deepening of Emma's disillusionment. He still retains the ability to 'talk nonsense very agreeably', however, and quickly recovers from the temporary lapse. His almost feminine fickleness, together with his rootlessness and blasé dilettanteism are opposed to the stability, splendour and traditional hospitality of Mr. Knightley's house. The trip to Box Hill is the best alternative that Emma can offer to 'a young man so much in want of change', and, after some hesitation, Frank agrees to accompany them.

The elegance of the party at Donwell is succeeded by the chaos and disintegration of the expedition to Box Hill. The harmony and order of the previous scene are broken up, and the party splits into groups; the Eltons; Mr. Knightley, Miss Bates and Jane; Emma, Harriet and Frank Churchill. It is Jane Austen's idea of hell, the nearest she gets to representing paradise lost, in this novel.

Since this scene is to involve the humiliation of Miss Bates and the delivering of Mr. Knightley's rebuke to Emma, one has to adjust one's point of view constantly, according to the degree with which one sympathises with the various characters. Miss Bates is described at length in the third chapter of the first volume, and the main point that emerges is that she is popular because she is friendly, ugly, stupid, harmless and helpless. She is also poor, but happy and not mean like Mrs. Norris in *Mansfield Park*. 'It was her universal good-will and contented temper which worked such wonders. . . . She was a great talker upon little matters, which exactly suited Mr. Woodhouse, full of trivial communications and harmless gossip.'[3] The unique quality of her speech seems to look forward in its imaginative evocation of chatter to the famous Anna Livia Plurabelle passage in James Joyce's *Finnegans Wake*,[4] where the talk of the gossiping women washing and drying clothes is recorded against the background of the river Liffey. In the speech of Miss Bates the twentieth century 'stream of consciousness' novel, which attempted to record one's random thoughts and feelings as they pass through one's mind, is fore-

[1] Chapter 27.   [2] *Persuasion*, Chapter 20.   [3] Chapter 3.
[4] Published separately, pp. 196–216 in the Faber edition.

shadowed. One is also reminded of the illiteracy of speech of Mrs. Malaprop in Sheridan's *The Rivals* (1775) and of the prosaic, rambling inconsequence of the dialogue of Juliet's Nurse (even when she is speaking in verse) which contrasts with the speech of the courtiers and the lovers. There is a character called Miss Milles, described in *The Letters*, (pp. 360–1, and 483), who seems to have provided Jane Austen with her immediate inspiration. Miss Larolles in *Cecilia* is the primary literary source.

Miss Bates, being poor and without opportunities of improvement, can be understood and forgiven, though, however amusing her company may be, she is unfit to be the friend of Jane Fairfax and an easy victim for the wit of Emma. She is a bore, yet she is modest, knowing that her trivialities are dull and her limitations amusing only because they confirm the superiority of the malicious. It is difficult to strike a just balance in one's reactions. She is affectionate and full of 'guileless simplicity and warmth',[1] almost like Chaucer's Prioress, in this respect, 'and al was conscience and tendre herte'. The chivalrous Mr. Knightley sends her mother and herself a sack of baking apples every year, and her function is partly to provide a test of other people's chivalry, forbearance and charity. Frank Churchill remarks that 'she is a woman that one may, that one *must* laugh at; but that one would not wish to slight.'[2] Emma attempts to defend herself by saying 'You must allow that what is good and what is ridiculous are most unfortunately blended in her.'[3] It is her conduct after Emma's insolence, the spirit of charity and forgiveness which she shows, that is responsible for the horror that Mr. Knightley expresses: 'I wish you could have heard how she talked of it—with what candour and generosity.'[4] It is her poverty and the fact that she had known Emma from her earliest years that make the mockery of the heroine so unusually ungenerous.

That we can retain sympathy with Emma after her brutality and cruelty is one of the greatest triumphs of Jane Austen's art. The incident is the climax of the process of self-deception (which is also self-betrayal) with which the novel has been concerned. Emma redeems herself by the immediate repentance (not made any easier by

[1] Chapter 33.   [2] Chapter 30.
[3] Chapter 43.   [4] Chapter 43.

Miss Bates's 'dreadful gratitude') in the following chapter. Mr. Knightley, the embodiment of liberality and candour, acknowledges the change: 'It seemed as if there were an instantaneous impression in her favour, as if his eyes received the truth from her's, and all that had passed of good in her feelings were at once caught and honoured. He looked at her with a glow of regard.'[1] It is because Emma has redeemed herself so completely that there is no taint of insincerity in her disposing of Frank Churchill, whose influence was largely responsible for the behaviour at Box Hill: 'None of that upright integrity, that strict adherence to truth and principle, that disdain of trick and littleness, which a man should display in every transaction of his life.'[2] Her indignation is modified by the thought that 'she was extremely angry with herself. If she could not have been angry with Frank Churchill, it would have been dreadful'.[3] As is the case with Marianne Dashwood in *Sense and Sensibility*, Catherine Morland in *Northanger Abbey* and Elizabeth Bennet in *Pride and Prejudice*, the scene of humiliation is the prelude to triumph. These heroines lose nothing, compared with Fanny Price and Anne Elliot, by being proved to be mistaken in their opinions and feelings.

The flirtation between Emma and Frank Churchill is no longer taken seriously by either of them when the Box Hill party takes place. They merely indulge in gallantry to escape from boredom. To others, the relationship still appears to be serious: the Eltons and Jane Fairfax regard it as such. The fact that Emma should laugh and generally be gay and thoughtless from disappointment, is a typically acute insight. Frank Churchill, himself, is in a mood verging on hysteria, and the party ends in a spirit of frustration and anti-climax. The rebuke of Mr. Knightley is quiet, brief and devastating. The difference between his friendship, with its unsparing stress on facts, however unpleasant, and the trivial flattery of Frank Churchill, could not be made more clear. There are few more effective denunciations of heartlessness than this short speech by the character who personifies everything that Jane Austen most respects.

The final complication is provided by Harriet, who, having rejected Mr. Martin and been rejected by Mr. Elton, now considers that she has hope of gaining the affection of Mr. Knightley himself.

[1] Chapter 45,   [2] Chapter 46.   [3] Chapter 47.

Emma, thinking that Harriet is grateful to Frank Churchill for rescuing her from the gipsies, learns that it is Mr. Knightley's gallantry
when he dances with Harriet, and thus rescues her from the contempt of the Eltons, that has transformed the protégée into a potential
rival.[1] There is a certain operatic flavour about the complications of
the intrigue at this point, that reminds one of a musical fugue rather
than of drama. After the ball, Harriet reveals to Emma the box of
precious treasure, which she is now determined to destroy, containing the small piece of court-plaister and the end of the old pencil,
previously used by Mr. Elton. The musical analogy is emphasised by
the resemblance to the scene in Mozart's *The Marriage of Figaro*,[2]
where Cherubino snatches the Countess's ribbon from Susanna, and
it is found tucked away in his sleeve at the beginning of the second
act. Harriet and Cherubino resemble each other in their youthful
innocence and inconstancy, though Cherubino is also lively, intelligent and mischievous. Harriet, brutally disillusioned by Mr.
Elton, is to be gently reconciled with Mr. Martin by Mr. Knightley.
She ends eventually where she began, as if at the conclusion of a very
elaborate dance.

It is the revelation of the secret engagement between Frank
Churchill and Jane Fairfax which leads to the clarification of the intrigue. The anxiety of the Westons, their reluctance to disappoint
Emma, are shown to be unnecessary, but the final exposure of Frank
Churchill's unworthiness, following Harriet's confession of her love
for Mr. Knightley and her reasons for hoping that it is returned, has
the inevitable result. Emma, at last, understands her own heart: 'It
darted through her, with the speed of an arrow, that Mr. Knightley
must marry no one but herself!'[3] At the same time, she realises how
her past conduct has been completely mistaken: 'With insufferable
vanity had she believed herself in the secret of everybody's feelings;
with unpardonable arrogance proposed to arrange everybody's

[1] Mr. Knightley's gallantry is an incident that originated in *The
Watsons*, the early fragment which Q. D. Leavis considers to be the
primary source of the novel.

[2] The opera is adapted, of course, from the French of Beaumarchais.
There is a similar incident described in *Jane Austen's Letters*, p. 412.

[3] Chapter 47.

destiny. She was proved to have been universally mistaken; and she had not quite done nothing—for she had done mischief. She had brought evil on Harriet, on herself, and she too much feared, on Mr. Knightley.' This insight into her own weaknesses and failings follows closely on the realisation of the baseness of Frank Churchill, and prepares the reader for the surrender of the imaginative heroine to the voice of reason, 'upright justice and clear-sighted good will.'[1] Just as Emma suffers the pain of self-knowledge, the apparent paragon of virtue, Jane Fairfax, endures the pain of confession and revelation of her past deception. Jane Fairfax is more accustomed to suffering, however, and her self-examination and self-condemnation have been continual since she consented to the private engagement.

The best that Emma can now expect is that Mr. Knightley will remain single and her friend. In this mood of discouragement, bordering on despair, Emma succumbs to a sudden nostalgic and retrogressive affection for her father, and decides that she would not marry even if asked by Mr. Knightley. This is her final self-deception, marking the most melancholy stage in the quick survey of her past relationships. Then the mood suddenly changes, and the return of hope coincides with a new appreciation of the beauty of the outside world. During Emma's sad, introspective evening at Hartfield, 'the weather added what it could of gloom. A cold stormy rain set in and nothing of July appeared but in the trees and shrubs, which the wind was despoiling, and the length of the day, which only made such cruel sights the longer visible'.[2] At the beginning of the next chapter, 'the weather continued much the same all the following morning; and the same loneliness, and the same melancholy, seemed to reign at Hartfield—but in the afternoon it cleared; the wind changed into a softer quarter; the clouds were carried off; the sun appeared; it was summer again'. This use of a scene, the emotional overtones of a place or a season, to represent a change in mood, frequently occurs in *Mansfield Park* and *Persuasion*, and rarely in the earlier novels. It adds a richness and mellowness to the analysis of manners and morals within a limited social group. No longer are human beings regarded as self-sufficient, or personal relationships considered separately from the world of nature. The changes and fluctuations of civilised life

[1] Chapter 48. [2] Chapter 48.

are those of nature itself, and the ideal human activity is to introduce order, grace and harmony into the world, as the landscape-gardener does.

The novel now moves naturally to its climax, Mr. Knightley's proposal to Emma. The emotional undercurrents and changes of tone in their conversation match the beauty and variety of the natural scene which introduces it. Their thoughts and reactions are quick, as befit two alert and intelligent people, yet beneath their changing moods there is serenity, the result of a long and enduring affection. Quiet and commonplace on the surface, still very much concerned with everyday affairs, the stresses and disagreements due to their relationships with other people, the dialogue delicately and sensitively explores the state of each other's feelings, and culminates inevitably with Mr. Knightley's question, 'Tell me, then, have I no chance of ever succeeding?' Behind this simple question, which does not appear at all sentimental or banal in its context, there is all Mr. Knightley's integrity and devotion, implicitly opposed to the duplicity of Frank Churchill. The reply of Emma is equally reticent and decisive: 'What did she say?—Just what she ought, of course. A lady always does.' The reconciliation provokes Jane Austen to one of the few passages of direct moralising: 'Seldom, very seldom, does complete truth belong to any human disclosure; seldom can it happen that something is not a little disguised, or a little mistaken; but where, as in this case, though the conduct is mistaken, the feelings are not, it may not be very material. Mr. Knightley could not impute to Emma a more relenting heart than she possessed, or a heart more disposed to accept of his.'[1] The epigrammatic quality of the writing and the brief concentration of the scene reflect the larger structural economy of the novelist at this crucial point in the story, and the flexibility as well as the control of the novelist is shown in the paragraph of exuberant comedy, immediately following the scene of the greatest emotional intensity. The intensity of emotion is dissipated and distanced with the sudden change into the earlier burlesque manner of the Juvenilia, *Sense and Sensibility* and *Northanger Abbey*, and with the revelation of the purely egoistic self-deception of the previously impeccable Mr. Knightley.

[1] Chapter 49.

It is interesting to compare Jane Austen's method of arranging the *éclaircissement* in the novels. In *Sense and Sensibility* it is sense that triumphs, and the emotional scenes of proposal are avoided at the end of the novel. In *Pride and Prejudice*, as a deliberate contrast with his earlier proposal, Darcy makes a brief declaration like Mr. Knightley, but the moment is without any of the intensity of the scene in *Emma*: 'The happiness which this reply produced, was such as he had probably never felt before; and he expressed himself on the occasion as sensibly and warmly as a man violently in love can be supposed to do.'[1] In *Mansfield Park*, Jane Austen winds up the story in the last chapter with an exaggerated light-heartedness and detachment which conceal embarrassment and lack of interest: 'I purposely abstain from dates on this occasion, that every one may be at liberty to fix their own, aware that the cure of unconquerable passions, and the transfer of unchanging attachments, must vary much as to time in different people.'[2] There is no equivalent in these novels to the sudden clearing of the air, the sense of emotional fulfilment that follows the resolution of a long misunderstanding and frustration, that occur in *Emma*: 'This one half hour had given to each the same precious certainty of being beloved, had cleared from each the same degree of ignorance, jealousy, or distrust.'[3] Even Frank Churchill describes a very similar experience in his letter to Mrs. Weston: 'We are reconciled, dearer, much dearer, than ever, and no moment's uneasiness can ever occur between us again.'[4] In *Northanger Abbey* the tone is cool and the attitude detached: 'I must confess that his affection originated in nothing better than gratitude, or, in other words, that a persuasion of her partiality for him had been the only cause of giving her a serious thought.'[5] The cancelled chapter in *Persuasion* comes nearest in its tone and mood to *Emma*. Jane Austen is again dealing with the theme of reconciliation after estrangement, and there is a depth of feeling and immediacy that had been unequalled in her work: 'all suspense and indecision were over. They were re-united. They were restored to all that had been lost. They were carried back to the past with only an increase of attachment and confidence. . . . And these precious

---

[1] *Pride and Prejudice*, Chapter 58.   [2] *Mansfield Park*, Chapter 48.
[3] *Emma*, Chapter 49.   [4] *Ibid.*, Chapter 50.
[5] *Northanger Abbey*, Chapter 30.

moments were turned to so good an account that all the most anxious feelings of the past were gone through.'[1] In the revised version of this chapter, the intensity and intimacy of the reconciliation are heightened still further: 'There they exchanged again those feelings and those promises which had once before seemed to secure every thing, but which had been followed by so many, many years of division and estrangement. There they returned again into the past, more exquisitely happy, perhaps, in their re-union, than when it had been first projected; more tender, more tried, more fixed in a knowledge of each other's character, truth, and attachment; more equal to act, more justified in acting. And there, as they slowly paced the gradual ascent, heedless of every group around them, seeing neither sauntering politicians, bustling house-keepers, flirting girls, nor nursery-maids and children, they could indulge in those retrospections and acknowledgments, and especially in those explanations of what had directly preceded the present moment, which were so poignant and so ceaseless in interest.'[2] After all her ironies, wit and satire, this is the central experience which seems to lie at the heart of Jane Austen's novels. It is, in a sense, an indulgence, a wish rather than a desire that one could expect to be fulfilled in ordinary life, an idealisation which the crudeness and clumsiness of everyday experience rarely allow to come true. It is the Paradise of Jane Austen's divine comedy.

The relationship between Emma and her father has in the past given dignity and usefulness to the heroine's character. One critic has suggested that Mr. Woodhouse is really the child. The comedy of the hatred of marriage which he shows becomes potentially tragic at the end. Despite the ridiculousness of her father's prejudice, the heroine still feels responsible for him, and bound to the old relationship. She is also bound to consider Harriet, who has been encouraged by her flattery, and is now under the delusion that Mr. Knightley returns her affection. Then, there is Frank Churchill's letter of explanation to be 'waded through', as Emma expresses it to herself, followed by Mr. Knightley's severe though impartial judgment on his character. The resemblance between Emma and Frank Churchill makes Mr.

[1] Published in R. W. Chapman's edition of the novels. See *Persuasion*, pp. 258–9.

[2] *Persuasion*, Chapter 23.

Knightley's opinion of 'the child of good fortune' (Emma's words, describing him) an implied criticism of the heroine. When reading Frank Churchill's letter it is made clear that Mr. Knightley passes quickly over those parts describing incidents which reflect unfavourably on Emma. Later, when the tension has subsided, Mr. Knightley directly suggests that she is as selfish as Frank himself. The severity of his judgment, in her case, is tempered by love, but it is firmly delivered: 'I am losing all my bitterness against spoilt children, my dearest Emma. I, who am owing all my happiness to you, would not it be horrible ingratitude in me to be severe on them?'[1] Perhaps Mr. Knightley is guilty of a slight cynicism here, a belief in the power of self-love as a motive for human action that looks back to Bishop Butler's *Sermons* and Pope's *Essay on Man*.

The story is rounded off with the reconciliation of Harriet and Mr. Martin, providing an ironic, comic contrast with that of Emma and Mr. Knightley. The revelation of the full details about Harriet's illegitimacy completes the deflation of Emma's illusions. The incident which persuades Mr. Woodhouse to agree to the marriage of his daughter to Mr. Knightley also adds to the comedy of the close. It is fear and not love that prompts him. The robbing of poultry-houses finally makes him give his consent. Mr. Woodhouse is something of a tame bird himself, and 'the strength, resolution, and presence of mind of the Mr. Knightleys, commanded his fullest dependance'. The very rhythms of the sentence bring the two brothers before us, in all their vigour. A last ironic touch is provided by Mr. Elton giving his blessing to the marriage, followed by the envious and ill-tempered comments of his wife. Yet, the irony is modified and deflected by the succeeding and final sentence, which suggests the triumph of nature against all obstacles, and the unity of the sensitive and intelligent with which *Pride and Prejudice* also concludes. The sensitive and intelligent form the 'band of true friends' whose smallness is Jane Austen's reason for taking such an astringent attitude towards society as a whole.

[1] Chapter 53.

Select Bibliography

BIBLIOGRAPHY

R. W. Chapman, *Jane Austen: A Critical Bibliography*. Oxford, 1953.

STANDARD EDITIONS

R. W. Chapman, *The Novels of Jane Austen*. The Text based on Colla-
tion of the Early Editions, with notes, indexes, and illustrations
from contemporary sources. In Five Volumes. Oxford, third
edition 1933.

Jane Austen's Letters, ed. R. W. Chapman. Second edition, Oxford, 1952.

Emma, edited, with an introduction, by Ronald Blythe. Penguin English Library, 1966.

BIOGRAPHY

J. E. Austen-Leigh, *Memoir of Jane Austen*, ed. R. W. Chapman. Oxford,
1926.

W. and R. A. Austen-Leigh, *Jane Austen, Her Life and Letters*. 1913.

Elizabeth Jenkins, *Jane Austen, a Biography*. 1938.

CRITICISM

Mary Lascelles, *Jane Austen and Her Art*. Oxford, 1939.

D. W. Harding, *Regulated Hatred: An Aspect of the Work of Jane Austen*,
Scrutiny, Vol. VIII, No. 4, March 1940.

Q. D. Leavis, *A Critical Theory of Jane Austen's Writings*, *Scrutiny*, Vol.
X, No. 1, June 1941.

R. W. Chapman, *Jane Austen: Facts and Problems*. Oxford, 1948.

Arnold Kettle, *An Introduction to the English Novel*, Vol. 1, 1951, contains an essay on *Emma*.

Marvin Mudrick, *Jane Austen, Irony as Defense and Discovery*. Princeton,
1952.

Andrew H. Wright, *Jane Austen's Novels: A Study in Structure*, 1953,
revised edition, 1961.

Lionel Trilling, *Jane Austen's Emma*, *Encounter*, Vol. VIII, No. 6, June
1957.

Robert Liddell, *The Novels of Jane Austen*. 1963.

W. A. Craik, *Jane Austen: The Six Novels*. London, 1965.

A. Walton Litz, *Jane Austen: A Study of her Artistic Temperament*. London,
1965.

GENERAL

J. M. S. Tompkins, *The Popular Novel in England, 1770–1800*, 1932.

Index